The

THIEF

in Your

COMPANY

The
THIEF
in Your
COMPANY

PROTECT YOUR ORGANIZATION FROM THE FINANCIAL
AND EMOTIONAL IMPACTS OF INSIDER FRAUD

TIFFANY COUCH
CPA/CFF, CFE

The Thief in Your Company

Protect Your Organization from the Financial and Emotional Impacts of Insider Fraud

ISBN   978-1-61961-586-1   *Paperback*

978-1-61961-587-8   *Ebook*

LIONCREST
PUBLISHING

To Dad

You believed when no one else did,
and that made all the difference.

*"It takes time for an acorn to turn into an oak,
but the oak is already implied on the acorn."*
—ALAN WATTS

Contents

Preface

I COULD NOT HAVE WRITTEN THIS BOOK OR IMPARTED THIS knowledge without the clients who have entrusted me and my firm, Acuity Forensics, with some of the most difficult situations they've faced in their professional roles. There are simply insufficient terms to express my gratitude for the opportunity to help them and their businesses. The stories within this book are all true. In order to protect my clients and their identities (not to mention, the fraudsters in this book), I have changed names, geographic locations, genders, and descriptions of the nature of their businesses. What has not changed are the nature of interactions, the nature of the fraud schemes or how they were uncovered, or the loss amounts.

You will not find much technical jargon in this book (if you do, you can find a glossary of terms in the back). This was purposeful. *The Thief in Your Company* is aimed at business owners and managers who may be new to the topic of fraud risk. If you are an auditor, fraud investigator, or educated business professional, please keep reading. My hope is that you will find ways to connect with your colleagues and clients on a human or emotional level, especially when fraud happens. I also hope that you will learn to continue to trust your gut. These two "soft skills" will be critical to the success of your engagements.

The success of this book and my client engagements is not the result of my sole efforts. This book could not have been made real without the cheerleading efforts of Katie Curry, Acuity's Media Director and this book's editor. She's the one who championed the idea that what we do at Acuity Forensics should be shared with a larger audience.

Brandon LeMay, my brother, came to work with me a few years ago so that I could get through what I thought was a "short period of being busy" and so that he could spend more time with his son. Turns out that Acuity was where he needed to be long-term. We've never stopped bringing work in the door and he continues to work side-by-side with me, turning data into information—information that results in our clients' ability to make better and more-informed decisions. Because of Brandon and his talents, Acuity helps more people. I couldn't ask for a better Analyst or a better brother.

Acuity would not be here but for my husband, Rusty Couch. He held the belief that starting my own business was the "only right way" even though he was a stay-at-home dad and I was the sole provider for the family, and there were no guarantees we would ever have clients. Rusty lets me follow where the fraud trails and speaking engagements lead, which typically lead far from home here in the Pacific Northwest or keep me working too late into many nights. His faith and strength provide a home base for me and our boys. I am eternally grateful for the privilege of being your wife.

Introduction

THE CALL I RECEIVED DAYS BEFORE CHRISTMAS WAS unfortunately similar to most of the calls I receive from new clients. The voice on the other end of the line was frantic. "Ms. Couch," a man said, "I need your help. I caught my new office manager stealing from me." I asked him to tell me more about the situation. How was this person caught? How new was she to the company? The man explained how the new manager was hired four months prior, and in that short amount of time she had begun to write $5,000 checks to herself.

Yet another likely fraud—another opportunity for me to unravel a complex financial puzzle, another opportunity for me to navigate a client through what will be one of the most difficult experiences in their business's history.

"I'm so sorry this is happening," I said to the caller. It's usually the last thing someone expects to hear from an accountant, but I have come to find—and it is my hope you will, too—that the emotional impact of fraud is usually greater than the financial toll.

He continued to tell me what had happened over the last four months—how she was hired quickly, and swiftly became an indispensable part of the company. When he told me that within weeks of her hire date, she was already comfortable enough to write herself checks for thousands of dollars, I said, "She's done this before."

"Wait," the caller said, "do you know her?"

No—I didn't know this woman in particular, but having investigated the actions of men and women just like her, I notice patterns. Most white-collar criminals utilize their likability and trustworthiness to perpetuate significant financial crimes against businesses and individuals. And someone who is comfortable enough to write large checks so soon is no amateur. This particular woman stole almost $10,000 in four months. When we presented our case to the police detectives, they confirmed that she had been arrested earlier that year for stealing from her previous employer. It was likely, they said, that she stole from my client to pay restitution back to them.

Why this book? Why this story and the many more that will follow? Because I have found that no organization is immune from the risk of fraud. It doesn't matter if you own a small, privately held business or if you are the director of internal audit for a large, publicly traded corporation—fraud can happen anywhere. I want to educate all businesses, big and small, that the best ways to prevent fraud are by being aware and vigilant—aware of the signs of financial fraud and vigilant about the simple and effective methods to detect and deter it.

If you find yourself in the position of needing to understand fraud risk in your organization and you want to avoid a similar fate in your company, you've come to the right place.

I am also writing this book for the countless victims of fraud— those who unwittingly covered for suspected fraudsters, those who spoke up and were ignored, and those who chose to pursue a criminal, civil, or insurance claim. This book is for those people, who felt their trust and good judgment were violated, and who felt alone in stages of shock, anger, sadness, and frustration. You are not alone—your feelings are normal, and you are definitely not crazy! Being a victim of fraud is not your fault. The stories mentioned in this book seek to illustrate that many have suffered the same fate, and many have since recovered, both financially and emotionally. Although fraud can feel like the lowest point of one's career, it can be overcome, appropriately dealt with, and the lessons learned can make an organization stronger.

I also seek to dispel a lethal myth among business owners and managers who are lulled into believing "fraud can't happen here." They reassure themselves with the following phrases:

- "We have great internal controls."

- "We have the best employees."

- "'Betty has been with me for years; she's part of the family.'"

- "Cash flow has been 'off,' but there must be another reason."

- "Our auditors give us a 'clean bill of health' every year."

The truth is, fraud can happen anywhere. Don't take it from me. According to the *2016 Report to the Nations on Occupational Fraud and Abuse*, published by the Association of Certified Fraud Examiners, on average, businesses lose 5 percent of their gross revenues from fraud. What would your organization do with 5 percent of gross revenues? Pay dividends? Reinvest in technology or more staff? Increase pay for employees? Fraud can be missed for a variety of reasons, but it is usually overlooked because business owners aren't looking in the right direction—they don't recognize the signs and often are not looking at the right culprits. The person who steals from an employer is almost always the most trusted and well-liked employee. It's usually the last person anyone would suspect.

One client of mine, a doctor, was someone I had come to know through my connections in our business community. He called me one afternoon, clearly embarrassed and distressed, and said, "I caught my long-term office manager giving herself more payroll than I authorized. I think she paid herself $20,000 more in payroll last year with no good explanation." He asked me to come in and write up the loss for an insurance claim.

The doctor had heard me speak on the topic of fraud prevention on multiple occasions. He heard me tell business owners that trust is not an internal control, and that the goal is to implement proper oversight over our employees and assets. When I arrived at the office, the doctor said, "I would come back from your talks and feel energized. I changed things in the office to make sure we had appropriate controls, but I never put controls around Judy." He shook his head. "I loved Judy. My patients loved Judy. She's been with me for more than a decade. I would have never dreamed she would do anything like this, and even though you always said the person you trust the most is the one who ends up stealing from you, I did not believe it could happen to me. I didn't think she could ever do such a thing. I thought she was the exception to the rule.

"Tiffany," he said with disappointment and sadness, "I thought I was immune to this."

I empathized. I told him how sorry I was that he had to call me about the situation. I encouraged him to tell me "everything," assuring him that his expression of emotion was normal. It's never fun to show up at someone's office to investigate fraud and ask him or her to reiterate all the painful details. However, those painful details often provide important clues about the case. I asked what else Judy had access to as an office manager. The doctor said that part of her job—in addition to payroll—was taking all of the money to the bank.

The office records quickly confirmed that Judy wrote herself more than $20,000 in extra payroll. Yet I found something even more problematic: evidence of a cash skimming scheme. It appeared that hundreds of thousands of dollars in cash from the doctor's practice never made it to the bank.

The doctor's initial reaction was one of disbelief. He wanted to know what I had looked at and how I was able to make such a claim in a fairly short period of time. He was incredulous. "Are you sure, Tiffany?" he pleaded. "Could there be another explanation?" I assured him that his patient records, receipting system, appointment calendar, and other documentation supported my findings. "You don't understand," he said, "I've heard you talk over and over again, and I still didn't think it could happen to me."

I have heard this heartbreaking story too many times to count. I have watched as people cry, blame themselves, blame others, and begin the long, slow process of healing. The heartbreak is not about the missing money. The heartbreak is about the unfathomable breach of trust made real. That's why fraud is such a devastating crime.

For more than a decade my entire accounting practice has focused on the investigation of financial crimes. That experience has helped me to uncover patterns—insights that I know will help those who are facing fraud, want to deter it, or who have already been through it. These patterns include the profile of a typical fraudster, the red flags that are most common in investigations, and the simple ways fraud can be uncovered.

The most surprising pattern I have seen is the emotional impacts fraud has on people—in organizations of all sizes. These emotional impacts often allow a fraud to continue for longer than necessary, and defer the investigation of accounting anomalies, for fear that an employee may be angered or offended.

The good news is, fraud can be prevented. There are easy steps to take to protect your assets, your business, and the well-being of your company and employees. The key is not to be afraid to talk about it, address it, and lead the charge to prevent it. This topic isn't as scary or difficult as it may seem. It won't cost a lot to implement systems and it doesn't require a more robust accounting team. In the long run, it will spare not only financial hardship but also the emotional turmoil and heartbreak left in the wake of financial fraud.

To those who are victims of fraud—either in the past or currently wondering if you are now—I want to say: I'm sorry. You are not alone. If you are feeling betrayed, angry, sad, or confused, these feelings are completely normal. Keep reading. Within these pages you will discover how fraudsters use their ability to be liked and to be trusted to perpetuate their crimes. You will also find that there are many other victims, like you, who have worked through these emotions, learned the facts, and brought clarity to their situation, ultimately discovering newfound strengths for their business and themselves.

PART I

The Second-Oldest Profession

Chapter 1

FRAUD IS A HUMAN PROBLEM

TOM, THE LONG-TENURED CFO OF MY CLIENT'S COMPANY who had recently been put on administrative leave, arrived unannounced and with his attorney. He sat quietly while his attorney told my client, Gary, that Tom borrowed more than $750,000 from the company. The attorney apologized on behalf of Tom, saying he was sorry Tom never told Gary about the loan. "Listen, Tom is truly remorseful. No reason to raise the flag any further, as Tom has every intention of paying the money back."

It was a curious start to a new case. Tom had been placed on administrative leave from Gary's company after it was discovered that Tom lied about a bad investment of $25,000 and left a suspicious $350,000 journal entry in the company's cash accounts. Then, Tom showed up unannounced with his attorney to say Tom had borrowed $750,000. Gary, his attorney, and his CPA were shocked when they heard Tom had borrowed such an extraordinary sum without informing anyone about what he had done. The loan had never shown up on the balance sheet or in any other financial report prepared by Tom. The CPA took Gary aside and said, "Something is not right. No one brings their attorney in unannounced and admits to a $750,000 loan that isn't on the books." He recommended that Gary call a forensic accountant in to take a closer look. Within forty-eight hours, I was on the case, absorbing more of the facts and trying to figure out whether these strangely specific, yet seemingly random, numbers contributed to a loss for the company. There were quite a few puzzle pieces, and I needed to figure out how they all fit together.

My client, Gary, was a farmer, through and through: he loved to be out in his truck and on the ranch, and was not someone who particularly cared to deal with numbers and financial reports. He had hired Tom to handle it. Tom worked as the company's CFO for more than twenty-five years—and was charged with all facets of the financial accounting, from budgeting to financial reporting, to investing the farm's excess funds based on the owners' investment parameters, and reporting the results on a monthly basis.

Years prior, unbeknownst to my client and the other owners, Tom invested $25,000 with a friend, outside of the owners' knowledge and investment parameters, and had lost the entire sum. Though $25,000 is a lot of money for most people, it was not a sizable amount for this investment pool. Still, Tom was in a pickle. He broke the rules, lost the money, and needed to figure out a way to report the loss on the monthly investment reports. Instead of admitting what he had done, he allocated the loss among other well-perform-ing investments. This allocation, or "plug number," was used for months and months to hide what had happened. He was able to hide the losses easily because he was the sole person in charge of both investing and reporting.

Unfortunately for Tom, part of the owners group hired a controller, Jason, to assist in the day to day accounting of the company. In order to take some of the workload off Tom and appropriately segregate duties, the owners thought it would be wise to train Jason on the investment reporting. Tom was put in the unenviable position of teaching the new controller how to compile reports—knowing he had been using a fake plug number to hide his loss.

Tom took Jason under his wing, befriending him, and explaining the investment report process. After Tom had gained Jason's trust, he came clean about the reason for the monthly $25,000 adjustment, but told him that it was really no big deal—that they could figure it out later. Jason, in turn, kept this secret for several months. He was new to the company, Tom was his mentor, and—most importantly—it was clear that everyone loved Tom. Jason didn't want to betray Tom's trust or rock the boat with management. Over time, though, Jason became uncomfortable keeping this secret from the owners. Eventually, his conscience got the best of him, and he went to management. He said, as far as he knew, "many years ago Tom invested $25,000 with a buddy of his and lost it, and now he's too afraid to tell you."

No one could believe that Tom would do such a thing. Gary was tasked with speaking to Tom about the potential anomaly. When Gary approached Tom with this new information, Tom acknowledged it as an error in judgment. Gary was furious. Up until that point, he never had cause to be concerned about Tom's performance or work ethic. He had hired Tom so that he could focus on the farm, which he loved, and trusted Tom to handle all of the accounting, investing, and financial reporting. He never imagined a situation like this. Not quite knowing how to handle it, Gary informed Tom that he needed to see not only the investment reconciliations, but all of the bank reconciliations as soon as possible.

Bank reconciliations are a pretty straightforward way for a company to ensure its accounting records match bank statements. The monthly reconciliation of the accounting records to the bank statements are standard operating procedure for most businesses each month. Unbeknownst to Gary, Tom had not reconciled the bank statements for the company for six years. In six years, no one had asked to see the reconciled bank statements, and Tom didn't bother to perform the task. For a company whose accounts show the flow of millions, sometimes tens of millions of dollars per month, being six years in arrears of reconciling the accounts would create a predicament for Tom. Understandably, Gary's request caused Tom to panic. Not wanting to raise any further suspicion, he promised Gary the reconciliations would be on his desk by Monday. He then worked the entirety of the weekend to reconcile those accounts—an enormous task. When his effort failed, he made a journal entry to cash, in the amount of $350,000, to force the company's accounts to reconcile to the bank statements. He placed the reconciliation on Gary's desk hoping he had dodged a bullet.

Gary reviewed the reconciliation report when he returned to the office on Monday. He noticed the $350,000 entry marked "JE" on the ledger report but did not know what it meant. He called his CPA and asked, "What does 'JE' mean? I thought bank accounts should only show deposits received and checks written."

The CPA said, "Typically that's true, but sometimes accountants need to adjust the books for certain transactions and we use journal entries to do it. JE means 'journal entry.' What's the amount?"

"$350,000."

Gary's accountant, properly stunned, said, "That makes no sense. There would be no reason to make a journal entry for that amount to your cash account."

You don't have to be a bookkeeper or accountant to know that something was awry. Gary's rudimentary understanding was right: money in, money out—for most businesses, that's all one should see in a cash account.

Gary called Tom into his office and immediately placed him on administrative leave pending further investigation into the journal entry. At this point, all he knew was that a $25,000 investment had gone bad and now there was a suspicious journal entry for $350,000 in the ledger. Understandably, he was upset, but given what he knew about Tom, he thought it was something they could reasonably resolve in due time.

The next day Tom showed up with his attorney and informed Gary about the $750,000 "loan." Within days, I was assigned to the case. My client tasked me with confirming the $750,000 loan and figuring out why it wasn't on any of the balance sheet reports.

The investigation revealed that at certain points in time the loans had actually been recorded on the balance sheet, but Gary had never noticed them because the reports Tom had provided had been high-level, summarized financial reports. For example, while the company might have multiple cash accounts, those cash accounts were summed up and reported as a single "Cash" figure on the financial reports. I found the "loan" account Tom had used to track his "borrowing," and discovered that this loan account, along with other legitimate company loans, was reported as a single item on the balance sheet, listed as "Loans Payable."

However, the transactions in Tom's loan account caused me concern. The $750,000 number Tom was giving to Gary didn't match the balance in the loan account. The loan account had a much lower number. A cursory review of the historical balance sheet reports turned up something else suspicious: I could see that the ending balances on one day were not always the same as the beginning balances on the next day.

A balance sheet is a snapshot in time. For instance, if I closed a shop tonight with $1,000 in the bank, tomorrow morning I would start with $1,000 when I opened. There is absolutely no reason for the beginning balances at the beginning of a day to be different than the ending balances that had been reported the night before.

A call to the software company confirmed that Tom had administrative privileges and their research provided proof that he had gone into the back end of the system and manipulated loan balances, effectively wiping loans off the books. I had learned how he had hidden the so-called loan and eventually written it off. Even though I was still unsure of the total amount, I was concerned. The fact was, I had quickly found more than one million dollars in "beginning balance" adjustments.

After confirming the existence of multiple checks made payable to Tom or his personal farm, typically in excess of $25,000 each, I felt confident that the transactions were likely not borrowings but instances of cash disbursement fraud. A legitimate loan would likely have a promissory note, signed by the owners, and would not be hidden in the books—it would be in the loan account. Furthermore, any write-off of the loan would be transacted through a journal entry, or actual payment, and would not have necessitated the back-end system adjustment. Tom had not followed any of these procedures. Instead, he hid the way the checks were entered into the accounting system, never informed management of the loans, and then wrote them off in various ways.

I brought my findings to my hotel room to confirm that there were no other explanations for what I was seeing. Honestly, I was actually a bit excited—I was looking at the largest fraud I had ever witnessed and knew there would be more to uncover. In hindsight, I can admit that my excitement was sort of perverse, given that this was causing so much strain and hardship for so many.

After two days of combing through reports and accounts, I bounded into my client's office with the financial reports and analysis in hand. I was certain I had explored all other avenues and there was no other explanation. This was no loan, and Gary had to know.

"Gary," I said, "this is not a $750,000 loan. In fact, with your lack of knowledge about its existence, the lack of a promissory note, the concealment of the transactions, and the subsequent write-offs, I don't see how this can be a loan at all. I've already found $1.2 million in transactions benefiting Tom, and I'm not done yet."

I grew up in a small town full of farmers, and it had always been my experience that farmers did not cry—it just wasn't in their nature. They were strong and stoic, they could handle anything, and they never displayed emotions in public. So, what Gary the farmer did next surprised me: he cried.

To me, this was an extraordinary response, and I was not entirely sure how to deal with the situation. After all, I was a "professional" and I was in the midst of a professional engagement. I felt like I needed to give him space, so I tried to make myself small and allow him to compose himself. Finally, he looked at me and said, "Tiffany, what are you telling me?"

I tried to repeat everything I had said, but words failed me. Instead, I offered only my sympathy. "Gary, I'm really sorry."

With tears in his eyes, he said, "You don't understand. Tiffany, if you're telling me that I can't trust Tom, then who can I trust? How do I even trust my wife?"

I was left speechless. No professional training in the world had prepared me for such a question. There's a misconception that fraud investigators only deal with numbers. It has been my experience that the reality of the job includes dealing with the emotional fallout. It was clear to me in that moment that his response had very little to do with the missing money, and everything to do with the previously unfathomable breach of trust. As an accountant—someone who perceived herself as a consummate professional—I felt wholly unprepared and unqualified to handle the situation. In that moment, Gary needed a psychologist, not me, the forensic accountant.

He explained to me that Tom had worked there for almost thirty years. Gary trusted him with bank accounts and investment portfolio and gave him a great six-figure salary. He added, "I gave him $10,000 for each of his kids, per year, to go to college. He had every benefit in the world. We played racquetball together, we've traveled with our wives together—for God's sake, he was the treasurer at our church. And you're telling me he's stolen a million dollars and you're not even done yet?"

"Gary," I said, "I'm so sorry. That's exactly what I'm telling you."

The lesson I learned from Gary that day was the single most important lesson I've learned in my career as an accountant and fraud fighter. And that lesson is this:

> *For fraud victims, it's not about the money. The crime of breached trust is more injurious than the missing funds.*

My experience with Gary taught me early on in my career that the impact of these crimes are more than the theft of money or assets. And a fraud investigation is more than a quest to figure out how much money was stolen. In the case of Gary's company, I realized that it wasn't about the millions of dollars I would eventually find missing—it was the fact that Gary trusted Tom implicitly with the money, taking a hands-off stance and focusing on the business instead. The money can often be recovered, but the violation of trust takes years to mend.

In the decade since that investigation, I have met countless fraud victims and learned that Gary's reaction was not an anomaly. I witness client after client experiencing the same strong emotional reactions. Upon realizing that fraud had occurred and that losses were often larger than initially assumed, the reaction almost always focuses not on the perpetrator or on the dollar losses but on this question: *"What's wrong with me, that I trusted this person?"*

In order to dispel the myth that "fraud can't happen here" one must first understand that fraud is not a money problem; it is a human problem. Fraudsters use their ability to be liked and to be trusted to perpetrate their crimes.

Think about it. Would you give access to your money, accounting systems, or intellectual property to someone you did not like or trust? Would you believe the financial reporting provided by someone you did not like or trust? Of course not!

And fraudsters know it.

So, what do they do? First, they become knowledgeable. Often, my clients find that fraudsters are the "go-to" people in the organization or department. Second, because of that knowledge, they become indispensable. Their importance to the organization rises. Very often, my clients are stricken with fear that these people may leave, taking with them processes, information, and relationships that are critical to the organization's daily function. Third, because of their knowledge and importance, they become friendly with management. Very often, they are described as being "favored" by owners, directors, or management. This status often equates to access. Sometimes it is unfettered access (e.g., an office manager or controller). Other times, they find ways to gain access (i.e., subvert internal control) without detection. The combination of their knowledge, importance, and access is a perfect venue for fraudsters to practice their craft. And the relationship fraudsters have with management and/or owners is the perfect "cover" for their crimes.

We have all been betrayed in our lives. Whether it was by a close friend, a spouse, a significant other, or a family member, we all know the devastating impacts that ripple through our hearts and our bodies. The physical and psychological reactions to these events can leave everlasting effects on our current and future relationships. In this regard, it is no surprise that my clients suffer acute emotional reactions upon hearing the news that fraud has occurred right under their nose, most often by someone I described above.

Few of us expect to be dealing with betrayal at the workplace. And certainly, none of us feel comfortable expressing the raw human emotions of sadness, anger, despair, or heartbreak at the office.

I am not a psychologist, but I've learned that doing my job well requires practicing compassion. Acknowledgment of the pain and confusion clients face—and assurances that these feelings are normal—is one of the first steps to take when dealing with fraud. Whether you are an auditor or investigator uncovering fraudulent behavior, or you are a business owner or CEO doing the same, understand that these emotions are normal. It's likely that nothing like this has ever happened to someone or their business before, and the initial shock brings most to tears—reflecting both sadness and anger. Most people unnecessarily apologize for their tears or their outbursts, especially as they are probably very professional in the workplace setting. Everyone—clients, employees, victims—need to give themselves space to process this information on an emotional level first.

Emotions, feelings, tissues, and hugs—probably not what one expects to read about in a book regarding fraud, and certainly not anything one expects to deal with as a professional. Those who have been taught to be the "consummate professional" may skip right over the feelings. We're often taught that feelings are not meant for the workplace; however, I have found that this simply doesn't work. Think about it. If fraud is a human problem, then shouldn't we first deal with it on a human level?

Connecting on a human level is not just an ethical consideration. As an investigator, it is critical to my case. When I express genuine concern, I find that this empathetic response allows for a closer, more trusting relationship with the client. This is incredible, given that the breach of trust my clients are dealing with is raw and new. However, by opening up to a sympathetic ear, my clients will often express relief and gratitude that they were able to get the information "out there" to someone who "believes them." What they don't know is that during the telling of their story (what I loosely call "therapy"), they are giving me clues. Clues about the potential suspects, clues about the tone of their company, access the person had, additional schemes they had not thought of, and potential interview subjects or even co-conspirators. Their therapy becomes my road map.

And the road maps my clients have courageously shared with me have all been lined with the gold that I now have the privilege of sharing with you.

CHAPTER 1 NOTES

Fraud is a human problem.

Fraudsters use their ability to be liked and to be trusted to perpetrate their crimes.

Trust is not an internal control.

Chapter 2

SIZE DOESN'T MATTER

ERIC WAS THE DIRECTOR OF INTERNAL AUDIT FOR A PUB-licly traded company in Silicon Valley and was informed that Deborah, the heir-apparent to the CEO, forged her boss's signature on expense reimbursement forms. On the phone, Eric said that everyone at the company was disappointed to hear that a woman with such a promising career path would make such a devastating decision. The company did not believe that the signature was forged for fraudulent purposes—they thought it was to expedite the reimbursement of her travel and company-related expenses. Charles, Deborah's boss and the CEO, requested an independent assessment of internal controls to ensure that such a thing could not happen again.

To say Deborah was successful was an understatement: she earned mid–six figures annually, traveled the world, sent her children to the best private schools in the region, and was clearly on track to be the next CEO. It seemed highly unlikely to everyone that Deborah was stealing money from the company.

It was so unlikely, in fact, that the purpose of our engagement was to "review internal controls" to "make sure this sort of thing couldn't happen again." An investigation was the last thing on my client's mind.

The first person my associate and I interviewed was Charles, the CEO. Though it was his signature that had been forged, Charles could not say enough good things about Deborah. He explained how Deborah worked her way up the ladder, rising in a mere ten years to her current position as chief technology officer. He loved Deborah like a daughter and secretly hoped she would be the person chosen to take over his job when he retired.

Then he told us how he had found out about the forgeries. For budgeting purposes, Charles had requested a list of technology expenses from the previous year. The CFO sent the list over, and when Charles saw that the top vendor in the technology department was Deborah, who had received expense reimbursements totaling $160,000, he called the CFO and said, "What do you mean Deborah is our number one *vendor*? I signed all of her expense reimbursement forms and I didn't sign $160,000 worth of expenses for Deborah last year. There is no way in hell that I did that." The CFO said, "Yes, you did. I'm looking at Deborah's reimbursement forms right here."

Charles asked to have all of Deborah's reimbursement forms sent to his beach house that weekend, and on Saturday morning, while he was still in his pajamas drinking his coffee, FedEx showed up to his home with a box, the size of which astounded him. In the box, he found expense reimbursement after expense reimbursement, all apparently bearing his signature. He told me during our interview, "I thought for sure that I needed to throw in the towel, that I must be getting dementia, because I did not remember signing most of those expense reimbursement forms."

He proceeded to do his very own bit of forensic accounting, carefully preparing two piles on the counter: one pile on the left for expenses he remembered signing, and one pile on the right for expenses he did not. When all was said and done, there was a pile of four or five expense reimbursements on the left, and about a ream's worth of paper on the right.

He e-mailed Deborah and asked, "Did I sign all of your expense reimbursements?"

Deborah answered within minutes. "Yes, you did."

Charles attached one of the suspected forged forms to an e-mail. "This signature is attributable to me, but I don't remember signing it. Can you explain?"

Deborah did not reply immediately. A few hours later, she e-mailed, "I don't know how to respond."

Charles said, "Well, tell me how you go about getting my signature."

Deborah responded with a long-winded explanation that amounted in the end to complete nonsense and was obviously not the truth.

At this point in the story, Charles stopped. Throughout the interview, he had been put-together and professional. He was smartly dressed, greeted us with cordial handshakes, spoke candidly, and answered our questions directly. Having finished telling us what happened, he said, "I'll go back to my office so that you can get back to work." Before he could leave, I said, "Tell me about Deborah, the person. Tell me about her—who she is. You told me how she is at work and how successful she's been, but tell me about Deborah."

He paused, considering the question. "Tiffany," he said, "you can see what everyone here wears to work. They're wearing jeans and T-shirts every day—nobody dresses up. But Deborah takes real pride in her appearance. She comes in to work every day in tailored suits." He continued to tell us that Deborah's children attended the most expensive private school in the region, and she had hopes that they would go on to attend Harvard or Yale. Instead of signing them up for basketball or volleyball, the children were involved in obscure and prestigious extracurricular activities or clubs that most kids hold no interest in. Every day, Deborah arrived at the office in either her high-end BMW or her Audi, and she made certain to park out front, ensuring that everyone could see what she drove. Charles said that Deborah came from a poor background and worked her way up the corporate ladder.

He suddenly became very quiet and opened his mouth as if he were about to speak. His hand moved to cover his mouth and he choked up. "I just don't understand how she could have betrayed me this much."

I handed Charles tissues, told him I was sorry he was going through this, and gently assured him that this reaction was quite normal. He apologized for his tears, became quiet, and clearly was lost in another thought. He chuckled, shook his head, and said, "Oh, never mind. I will let you ladies get back to it." Though I wanted to give him his space to clear his head and compose himself, I did not want to let him get away with saying, "Oh, never mind." When a client says that, there is usually a crucial piece of information that they feel is unimportant or too embarrassing to tell me about.

"What was in that 'never mind'? What were you thinking just now?"

He said, "I just don't get it. Deborah had the ability to approve accounts payable up to $50,000, meaning all expenses up to $50,000 could be approved by her without any other authority. All of these expenses on her reimbursement forms could have run through Accounts Payable with one strike of her own pen and without ever needing my signature. Why would she run these costs through her expense reimbursement forms and forge my signature? It just makes no sense to me. I'll never understand how this could happen."

He composed himself, thanked us for our time, and offered us any help we might need before he left us alone to work. After he was gone, my associate looked at me and said, "We're at this large publicly traded company and the CEO is emotional."

We sat and looked at each other, realizing that we had stumbled onto something important. I said "It's the same. The size of the company doesn't matter—the emotional reaction is the same."

When I first started Acuity Forensics, most of my clients were small and medium-size business owners, non-profits, and churches. That was my niche, and within those spheres I saw these emotional reactions over and over again. As a small business owner myself, I understood why. People start these ventures in their garage or in my case, a small home office, because they care deeply about whatever it is they're doing and want to make a difference. After some time, the business grows—they rent an office space, hire employees, train new staff members, watch as revenue grows along with the complexity of the business and its obligations. Starting a small business is a lot like having a baby: you dream about it, care for it, raise it, work through the growing pains, and suddenly your baby grows up and barely resembles the dream you held so long ago in your own two hands. Your company is your heart walking around outside of your body.

It's understandably devastating when someone takes that trusting, beating heart and twists it for his or her own gain. I initially thought that the reason I saw very emotional reactions to fraud was because my client demographic was largely made up of small business owners. As my business grew and I took on larger companies as clients, I found the reactions to fraud were always the same. The emotional response to these situations had nothing to do with the size of the business.

Charles's company had every internal control in place— auditors, checks and balances—and yet someone was able to manipulate the system and circumvent those controls. During that first interview, no fraud was suspected. Yet, Charles was emotional; his tears were a result of the betrayal of trust.

The information in Charles's "never mind" proved to be a huge clue to this fraud investigator. Why would someone who had the authority to approve accounts payable expenses up to $50,000 run smaller amounts through an expense reimbursement process that required her boss's signature? That didn't make sense. What also didn't make sense was that many of these expenses were for travel that didn't match Deborah's calendar. Our internal control review converted to a fraud investigation the same day. During the course of our investigation, we discovered that not only were Charles's signatures forged, the receipts attached to those forms were fakes as well. Deborah had perpetrated a fraud in excess of $1 million against that company by submitting fake receipts.

On the other side of the spectrum, a married couple who owned a business in a small town called me to investigate some curious items found on their company's bank statements. There was a DISH Network bill being paid through their account, but they didn't have DISH Network as their cable TV provider. When they called the company to ask whose account it was, they were given the name of their bookkeeper. They dug a little further into the bank statements and noticed that each month there was a Verizon Wireless bill being charged to them, even though both of them used AT&T. Finally, they confronted the bookkeeper, Sienna. A woman in her mid-twenties, Sienna initially said that she didn't know anything about it, but later explained that it was an accident.

The couple called their accountant, who directed them to me. I pored over their bank statements and found $1,250 in losses. When I showed this to the owners, they were shocked.

"It must be an accident, right? She must have done this accidentally."

I asked, "Have you ever paid a bill online, or bought anything on Amazon?"

They said yes.

"Walk me through what you have to do when you check out."

"Well," they said, "you have to put your name in, plus the address, which has to match the billing address for the card."

"Exactly," I said. "What else?"

"You type in the credit card number, the expiration date, and then flip the card over for the three-digit code on the back."

I nodded. At each and every step, Sienna had to know my clients' names, addresses, the credit card number, expiration date, and CVV code. The bookkeeper did this with multiple different vendors: her utility bills, her cable television bill, and her cell phone bill. Taking that tedious process into consideration, I asked them, "At what point is that an accident?"

The wife began crying. She said, "I never thought of it that way. You are right. This wasn't an accident. So, what is wrong with us, that we let this happen? She stole $1,250 from us and we believed her story. We just wanted her to pay it back and then give her a second chance."

When I interviewed the bookkeeper, she confessed, and was subsequently fired. I wrote up a report, and when I left that day, the husband and wife were crying together. This was a devastating loss for them. They only had ten employees, and they thought the world of their bookkeeper—a young woman, full of potential, whom they trusted implicitly. Now, they felt terrible having trusted her. The devastating loss was not the $1,250—it was that someone they had hired, adored, and trusted had stolen from them.

Though these two cases may look dissimilar at first, they actually have a lot in common. When Charles the CEO found out that Deborah was reimbursed for $160,000 in expenses the previous year, he was in disbelief. He called the CFO and said it couldn't be so because he hadn't signed that many reimbursement forms. Even when he was confronted with a box of reports bearing his signature, Charles could not believe that Deborah had forged his signature because she was stealing. He thought it was more likely that he had dementia, or that Deborah forged the signature to expedite reimbursement. When the husband and wife found out that the payments on their bank statements to vendors that were not their own totaled $1,250, they didn't want to believe it. They tried to rationalize: it was an accident, just like the bookkeeper had said.

Every client will try and rationalize why the person in question could not possibly be stealing. Every client will insist that there must be some other explanation for what's happening. It is not uncommon for me to hear that clients feel uneasy— they know something's not quite right, but they can't put their finger on it. In fact, many will tell me that the uneasiness has gone on for months, sometimes longer. Every client wants to find another way around the situation—whether it's an accident, just a lapse in judgment, or a clerical error. Regardless of the size or scale of the company or the loss, these rationalizations are the same. But most importantly, so too are the emotional impacts. Usually, the person stealing from the company is the one who is the most adored and trusted by the CEOs and owners. When someone steals from you or your company, whether it's $1 million or $1,250, it's a huge betrayal of trust. It's devastating and heartbreaking when you let someone into your circle of trust and she takes advantage of you. This is the very real human impact of fraud.

CHAPTER 2 NOTES

The emotional reaction to fraud is the same, no matter the size of the company.

If you find yourself in the corporate world dealing with the impact of fraud, do not be afraid to deal with the human elements first.

Strong emotion can often lead to information. Information can help provide clues for your case.

Chapter 3

DENIAL—NOT A RIVER IN EGYPT

THERE IS A SMALL POSTAGE STAMP OF A TOWN ON THE coast of Oregon with no more than two hundred and fifty residents. City hall is open only two days per week, and each month the city sends fewer than one hundred utility bills. When the mayor called me, the town was already several years behind in its audits, which were supposed to be remitted to the secretary of state's office annually. The mayor was concerned because it was partly his responsibility, but each time he approached the city clerk, Nancy, she would say that she didn't have the time or couldn't coordinate schedules with the CPA. There was always an excuse.

Other things were happening in the town that did not make sense. Every year, the council was told that they had less and less money for the budget. People complained that their utility bills were showing incorrect balances. The mayor would pay his utility bill in cash, but didn't always receive a receipt for the payment. Things just weren't quite right.

Meanwhile, people noticed that Nancy spent a lot of time at the local bar, playing video poker. It wasn't a crime, but it was a small town and people talked. Everyone knew she worked part time for the city, and it seemed odd that she had enough disposable income to sit down and play video poker each night.

The mayor heard that I had worked with a client in a neighboring town, helping them investigate missing money and eventually recasting their financial statements for their annual audits. He really wanted to bring me in to double-check the books to "make sure everything was okay." The city council pushed back, saying that they didn't want to step on Nancy's toes. The general consensus was that it was a small town with few resources, and Nancy was doing the best she could. For months, the city council said no, worried that my presence would hurt Nancy's feelings and make her feel inadequate.

Every few weeks, the mayor called me with yet another red flag, including the lack of basic financial reports to the city council, more complaints about utility billing errors, and Nancy's increasing agitation when questions were asked of her. I gave him advice where and when I could, but there wasn't much I could do until I properly looked over their books. Finally, as the next audit cycle approached and Nancy stalled in scheduling with the CPA firm, I suggested that the mayor ask the city council to bring me in to help prepare the books and records for the audit so that Nancy could focus on her day-to-day tasks. With that as the message, the mayor was able to get enough votes to have me come in for one day to see where they were on their audit and to verify that no money was missing.

I knew that Nancy had total control of all the money coming into the town. It was her responsibility to receive it, collect it, count it, put it in the accounting system, and take it to the bank. It was her job to write all the checks, mail them to vendors, and reconcile the bank accounts. She was also responsible for putting together financial reports for the city council, a task that had gone undone for months. The lack of financial reports was red flag number one.

The first thing I asked Nancy for was access to the electronic accounting system. I wanted to know if she used QuickBooks or any other accounting software to record the city's financial transactions. She told me that she kept the city's books on Microsoft Excel. Red flag number two: she didn't even have a traditional accounting software program. However, the Excel spreadsheet would suffice.

"Great," I said. "Can I see your Excel spreadsheet?"

She took her time. She walked around the office. She stared blankly at her computer screen. She went outside to smoke a cigarette, and I saw her hand shake as she lit it. She finally put the information on a thumb drive and handed it to me. When I opened up the file I could see that nothing had been entered into the spreadsheet for more than a year.

A definite dead end.

The mayor had mentioned that people were having issues with their utility bills. When people receive bills that say they have a balance but they know they've paid, that could be an indication that someone is skimming money and not posting payments to customer accounts. The mayor also mentioned that he paid his bill in cash each month but didn't receive receipts. I retrieved the bank deposit books—the ones that tell you to list the currency, coins, and all the checks you're depositing to the bank that day—and found that not one single, solitary coin or dollar bill had been deposited by the town in months. It appeared that only checks were being deposited. If the mayor made his utility bill payment in cash, there would surely be cash to deposit. But, I needed to figure out how to prove just how much revenue had come into the city or determine if the cash was lying around the office somewhere.

Not wanting to create more agitation for Nancy, I put the curious deposit tickets on hold and turned to the canceled checks. I wanted to verify whether Nancy had been writing checks to herself or any of her personal vendors. Though I did not see any problems with the checking account in terms of misuse of funds, there was something else missing: there were no checks to pay payroll taxes. I combed through every bank statement and every check. Going back two and a half years, I confirmed that there had not been any electronic payment or checks issued to pay state or federal payroll tax liabilities. Red flag number three. Unpaid payroll taxes are often a red flag that fraud is occurring. When cash is stolen, it can cause significant cash flow problems to the business. But one can only go so long not paying rent, utilities, or payroll. Not paying those expenses will be caught quickly. However, one can go years not paying IRS payroll taxes, as long as one can hide the mailed notifications the IRS will send.

I asked if I could look at the payroll tax forms, and Nancy told me they were in her car. She did this a few times—said something was in her car, spent quite a bit of time outside, and then returned with only a few sheets of paper. I asked why she kept documents in her car, and she said she sometimes worked from home. The rest of the payroll tax forms were in a filing cabinet, she said, but all I could find were historical payroll tax forms for periods of time before she had been employed at the city.

The last curious finding was a deposit slip in the book for several thousand dollars, but I could not trace the funds to the bank account. When I asked her why, she said all the money was at her house.

All of this occurred well before noon. At this point, I asked the mayor to meet with me so we could go over my preliminary findings. I indicated to him that I thought it would be necessary to interview Nancy regarding the situation. When we sat down with her and began asking questions, she became angry, called both of us horrible names—the likes of which shouldn't be repeated in print—and ran to her car. She peeled out of the gravel parking lot, leaving a trail of dust, and the mayor and I standing there, stunned.

By the end of my investigation, I confirmed that the city was three years in arrears in audits, more than two years behind in payroll tax filings and payments, and that Nancy had been pocketing the city's cash deposits for years. It was a classic cash skimming scheme, where any cash payments made to the city—utility payments and other city fees—were pocketed. We were able to prove the cash skimming scheme because Nancy had used a receipt book for some of the payments and had marked whether the funds had been received via cash or check. The cash was never deposited, while the checks were. This scheme went on for several years before the mayor called me.

Generally, by the time people have called me, they've resigned themselves to the fact that there is no other explanation for the missing money. Still, some small part of them wants to think there is another reason. The CEO rationalized that his employee forged his signature on expense reports in order to expedite reimbursements. The owners of a small business thought that payments for bills and accounts that didn't belong to them were an accident.

Most on the town council had a reason for why the audits weren't completed each year and why the utility bills weren't quite right. The mayor had known all along that there was something wrong because there were too many red flags: the annual audits and monthly financial reports went undone, utility bills were full of errors, and the part-time city employee in charge of the money played a lot of video poker. The mayor had a sense that something wasn't quite right. Yet everyone was able to come up with a million reasons why it couldn't be fraud:

- Maybe she's just overwhelmed; there's too much work to do.

- She just doesn't have time to get this to me.

- The books are just a little messy; it's no big deal.

- We just have a bad bookkeeper.

- She's a nice lady; she wouldn't do anything harmful.

And the biggest concern of all: "What will people think of me if I accuse Nancy of perpetrating a fraud or bring a fraud investigator in here?"

These rationalizations are all too common and are often the reason fraud schemes go on much longer than necessary.

According to the Association of Certified Fraud Examiners' *2016 Report to the Nations on Occupational Fraud and Abuse*, the median duration of a fraud is 18 months; with nearly one-third of frauds lasting at least two years before they were detected[i]. I can confirm within my own client experiences; this fact is true. What's more, the longer a fraud goes undetected, the greater the losses turn out to be.

MEDIAN LOSS BASED ON DURATION OF FRAUD

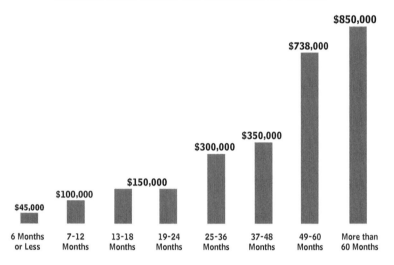

Source: ACFE 2016 *Report to the Nations on Occupational Fraud and Abuse*, Figure 18, Page 17.

The thing is, most of us are nice people. We get up every day, head off to work, do our jobs well, and follow the rules. If we find a wallet in a department store, we return it. Most of us don't sit around imagining how to steal from an employer. As such, that mindset often means that we can't fathom those who not only imagine perpetrating a fraud but actually carrying one out. We ignore common red flags: bad bookkeeping

---

i   Association of Certified Fraud Examiners (ACFE), *Report to the Nations on Occupational Fraud and Abuse*, p. 18.

or messy books, payroll taxes not being paid, business owners posting more revenue but somehow taking home less money, financial reports delayed or not provided because an accountant or bookkeeper is "too busy," and customers complaining about billing statement errors.

Circumstances like this can go on for years without further investigation. It often becomes part of the corporate culture—a "that's just the way it is" attitude. This is a kind of coping mechanism that people think is easier to deal with than confronting a difficult or problematic situation. Even when evidence is placed in front of them, clients will often rationalize or find acceptable explanations for our findings. Every client wants to give his or her employees the benefit of the doubt and try to find plausible reasons that do not include fraud or theft. It is human nature to want to assume the best from the people we trust. Sometimes, when someone decides to finally look into the matter, there will be pushback from other board members, co-owners, or employees. Even though everyone's stomach kind of aches with the knowledge that something isn't quite right, no one wants to believe the worst about someone he or she works with.

It is not uncommon that those who wish to look into it, like the mayor, are ostracized for speaking up.

Denial can go on for a long, long time, and as long as people are in denial, the fraud will continue—oftentimes for longer than it should. The more time passes, the more it allows for new and inventive ways for perpetrators of fraud to hide documents, distort the numbers, and destroy evidence.

Sometimes, the denial is so thick that the rest of the community becomes vitriolic toward those attempting to get to the bottom of the situation. People are so convinced by the outward character of the accused that they will ignore all the evidence to the contrary. There is one story that illustrates this so perfectly that it's almost too unbelievable to think true. Most people want to believe that they are rational, and that they wouldn't react in such a way if they had been presented with the same situation.

The case involved a bookkeeper of a small private school in California. The school was established more than a century ago and remained an excellent institution to educate primary school children. The school had a great reputation in the community. The bookkeeper, Barbara, was well loved and in her many years of employment at the school, always went above and beyond. Barbara sat in the classrooms if a teacher needed an aide. She helped out with the janitorial side of things, cleaning and repairing things that needed to be fixed. She volunteered for fund-raising projects and school events. She was positively adored by the students, their parents, the administration, and the board of directors. Everyone agreed that you couldn't find a better employee.

One day, the principal received a call from an IRS agent, who wanted to know why the school had not paid payroll taxes in several years. The principal had no idea what the agent was talking about—it was the first she had ever heard of it.

When I tell this part of the story to a room full of accountants, I ask, "How long does it take for the IRS to call your clients?" All accountants will tell you: a really, really long time. Few can even imagine an IRS agent actually calling a client. If you don't pay your taxes, the IRS will send letter after letter after letter after letter. Over time, the wording of them may escalate, but they will not call you for years. A call or visit from an IRS agent typically has to reach a point where, not only have you never made a payment, but you have also never filed a form, replied to a letter, or made contact with them in any way. A call from an IRS agent is a significant event.

It's not the job of the principal to pay the payroll taxes, but the head of a small private school would certainly know if the payroll taxes had gone unpaid for years. Such a situation would have been on financial reports, would have been part of the annual budgeting process, and certainly would have been discussed during board meetings. This principal was shocked at the news, and went straight to Barbara after she hung up the phone.

"I just received a call from the IRS," she said. "What's going on with the payroll taxes?"

Barbara was silent. Finally, she stammered, "It's true, I haven't paid the payroll taxes, and it's because we're running out of money. I haven't been able to tell you—the school is on the verge of bankruptcy!"

The principal was stunned. She called an emergency board meeting for that very evening, where Barbara told the board, in between sobs, "I'm so sorry. I have not paid the payroll taxes in three years." It was like the air had completely been sucked out of the room. She continued. "I was just trying to keep the school open. I just wanted to be able to make payroll for the teachers and pay the rent and keep the lights on. I stopped paying the payroll taxes because we didn't have enough money. I kept thinking I could catch us back up but it just never happened. I'm so sorry. I only wanted to save the school from going under."

Many believe the following reactions by the stunned board members and principal cannot be true.

I assure you that it is.

That evening's board meeting was remarkable. The board members and the principal cried as well, and got up from their seats to console Barbara. Some hugged her, and many even thanked her for saving the school. They all expressed that they were so sorry she had carried this burden for so long. They said it would never happen to her again and that they would make sure that somebody was always looking at the bank statements and the canceled checks and making sure that the bills were paid. Help, they said, was on its way.

In upholding this promise, they realized that Barbara was the only one writing checks, so they instituted internal controls— from then on, someone else would sign the checks and review the bills to be paid. Aside from that new control placed upon her, everyone continued to express their gratitude to Barbara for saving the school and making sure that everything else was taken care of, like the utilities and teacher's salaries.

The parents and the board rallied around the issue. The school raised a significant amount of money in a short period of time. They took every last dime out of the savings account and paid the payroll taxes, penalties, and interest. James, one of the parents who was also an attorney, sued the IRS—pro bono on behalf of the school—to get the penalties and interest abated and/or refunded. He argued that this lapse had been an anomaly; the school was running out of money.

Two years passed, and as this litigation proceeded, Barbara had to be deposed by an IRS attorney. James was present during Barbara's testimony, where she said something that, unbeknownst to the IRS agent, was a lie. James knew it immediately but waited to consult documents in the office. Sure enough, he could prove that Barbara had lied during her deposition. That was when he called me.

"I just don't feel comfortable with her story. I feel like somebody should just take a look at the books to make sure there is no money missing."

I told him to go back two years and find the bank statements and canceled checks for that period of time when she was not paying the payroll taxes and had total control over the checking account and to send those to me.

It's always like Christmas Day for me when I get new documents, but this was like ten years of Christmases. I do a lot of work for churches and private schools and the sheer number of bank statements for this small school was extraordinary. I started by parsing out all of these bank accounts. There were more than a dozen for this private school. Red flag number one.

At first, I only looked at the front of these bank statements, where I saw ATM withdrawal after ATM withdrawal. Now, no school that I've ever worked for has had ATM withdrawals, let alone that many. What school needs to withdraw cash via an ATM machine multiple times per week? None. Period. Red flag number two.

Then I looked through some of the canceled checks and saw $1,000 here and $2,000 there, all checks written to Barbara, in excess of her regular payroll checks, which I also found. These checks were written at erratic intervals—sometimes multiple checks in one day, all of which seemed to have been filled out by her but signed by someone other than Barbara. Did I potentially have a co-conspirator? Red flag number three.

I only had to view these bank statements for an hour before

I was ready to call James. I asked him, "Why would the school need an ATM card for cash withdrawals?"

There was a brief silence before he said, "They wouldn't, Tiffany. It's a school."

"Why would Barbara be writing checks to herself? Or rather, who would be writing checks to Barbara, outside of her payroll?"

"Well, they wouldn't be. Are you telling me that she is embezzling money from the school?"

"Potentially, yes," I said. "It looks like it. Unless these are reimbursements or draws on future payroll checks, then embezzlement is certainly a possibility. I'm not seeing large even-dollar deposits on the bank statements and her payroll checks are consistently the same amount, which indicates that these other checks are not likely draws on payroll."

I arranged to visit the school. The investigation eventually uncovered a cash disbursement scheme between $35,000 and $40,000 that we believed Barbara perpetrated by writing checks to herself and withdrawing cash from ATMs. As a result of our initial findings, Barbara was put on administrative leave.

As this was a small town and a small school, word about Barbara's leave got out immediately. I started getting phone calls from irate parents and staff, even a board member's wife—all accusing me of a witch hunt. "How dare you conduct this investigation!" they yelled. "This is unfair! Whatever you're saying is wrong." I have never experienced anything like it before or since. These people loved Barbara that much and were that upset that I was being hired to investigate her.

What made the whole situation even more incredible was the fact that this was not the first time Barbara had been investigated. She was accused of embezzling money from her prior employer, and the entire school community had supported her through that ordeal. The principal, parents, and staff attended her trial, and many rallied together to donate their time off to ensure she would be paid while she was out of work and on trial. Nobody believed that she could be capable of something so appalling.

With Barbara on leave under the current circumstances, there was no one who knew how to do the accounting. The school secretary was completely out of sorts. One day I walked into the school and found her waving around $800 in cash. She didn't know what to do with it. She said, "Tiffany, I need help. These parents came in to pay tuition, and I don't know what to do."

I sat down with her and said, "Okay, I'm good with Quick-Books. I'll show you how to post a payment. What's the student's name?"

She told me the name, and I searched for it in QuickBooks, but the child's name was not in the system. "No wonder you're having trouble," I said. "Maybe it's under the parents' names."

I did a search in QuickBooks for the parents' names, but they were not there either. I laughed and said, "Oh, no wonder you're having such a hard time. They're not in QuickBooks at all. They must be a new family. We need to get them set up as a customer so that we can post the payment for tuition."

She crooked her head to the side and furrowed her brow. "This boy is an eighth grader and he's been here since kindergarten," she said. "What do you mean he's not in QuickBooks?"

I looked from her to the $800 cash she held in her hands and said, "Let me guess, these parents pay cash every time?"

"Yes, they do! Sometimes, they come in and they pay for all three of their kids at the beginning of the year. Once, they brought us something like $10,000 cash just to pay their tuition for the whole year."

I asked her for the deposit slips, which she found in a drawer and brought back to the desk. I flipped through the two or three books that together spanned more than a year, and during that time there had never been one single penny or dollar in cash deposited to the bank. The only thing listed on those deposit slips were checks.

If you have kids who go to school, or if you remember what it was like to be in elementary school, you may recall that in addition to tuition, there are a lot of other fees: school lunch money, field trip money, fund-raiser money, band fee money, T-shirt money, extra-curricular clubs or sports fees. The list is endless. Schools—especially private schools—are almost always handling cash.

I ran an audit trail report in QuickBooks, where I found thousands of dollars of deleted tuition payments. Barbara had given parents receipts and then deleted everything out of QuickBooks so there would be no record. I called James and said, "She's not just writing checks to herself; she's skimming cash as well." We thought we were looking at a $40,000 fraudulent disbursement scheme. When I had completed the investigation, I had identified more than $200,000 in losses resulting from a cash skimming scheme of tuition money.

It should be noted that the only thing I was able to prove was the missing tuition, as there was no way to prove how much band money, lunch money, and fund-raiser money went missing over the years.

As the evidence against Barbara mounted, amazingly, so did the pushback I received. The love that these people had for Barbara absolutely blinded them. When I interviewed the volunteer mom, whose job it was to sign the checks, I showed her the checks Barbara had written to herself that were signed in this woman's name. Her husband, a CPA and board member at the time, sat with us during the interview. As I slid the pieces of paper across the table, she pushed them away, as if she couldn't stand to look at them or touch them. "You're wrong. You made those up," she said.

I asked, "How many checks have you written to Barbara?" She said, "None." She was beside herself with anger: "How dare you blame me! How could you say these things about Barbara? She would never do something like take the school's money."

I said, "You either wrote these checks to her or she forged your name. You've got to tell me the truth because these checks cleared the bank with your signature on them and Barbara cashed them."

Her husband, who had sat quietly the entire time, turned to her and said gently, "There's no other reason for these. These checks cleared the bank. Tiffany can't make these up."

The woman burst into tears. "I didn't write these checks. And my name is not forged. Barbara would tell me how busy she was and she'd hand me blank checks and I would sign them for her because I trusted her. We were all just so busy. She was my friend and I never thought anything of it."

Her heartbreak was palpable. She had loved this woman. It took a long time for her to look at those documents and really process what she was seeing. Even when the evidence was right in front of her, it was hard for her to come to terms with the fact that her trust in this woman had been so completely betrayed.

Barbara had used her abilities to be liked and trusted to perpetrate her fraud. She convinced everyone at the school that the charges brought against her by her previous employer were the result of "mean people." She had convinced them that anomalies related to the non-payment of taxes were a result of decreasing cash flow. After the board meeting where they hugged and cried, Barbara returned to her post as bookkeeper and found new ways to steal (the check writing stopped the day of the board meeting, yet there were no cash deposits made after that time). Meanwhile, the school community stood by her side through that trial as well as the deposition and investigation that ensued at the school. Understandably, it was difficult for them to reconcile the duplicitous nature of her actions. All they had seen was a sweet, responsible, and loyal woman whom they felt had been wrongly accused.

This story illustrates how difficult it is for kind, reasonable people—whether they are managers or owners of a business, board members, friends, or family—to wrap their heads around what is happening during a fraud. They would much rather believe whatever the thief says or what their eyes have seen. Or they will fill in the gaps themselves, coming up with other reasons to explain the anomalies they are finding. They will go to great lengths before admitting that their organization might be hemorrhaging cash because someone is stealing from them.

Denial and rationalizations allow problems to worsen or frauds to continue within organizations of all sizes. Fraudsters are counting on those denials and rationalizations and in fact, will be emboldened to escalate their schemes.

CHAPTER 3 NOTES

When dealing with a situation where multiple red flags are present, including:

- Lack of financial reporting;
- Bills not being paid;
- Customer billing error complaints;
- Persons with too much control over a process;
- Cash flow issues do not make sense when sales activity has increased;
- Pushback by person with control over the process.

...it is common to find rationalizations for and/or denial of a problem. Addressing the problem typically equates to addressing an individual and it is easier to work around the problem than it is to confront it.

Find ways to address the issue by obtaining the sufficient, relevant documents that will help decision makers identify whether there are clerical errors, a personnel issue, or fraud. Subsequent chapters will address specifics on where to look and documents to retrieve.

Part II

Right Under Your Nose

Chapter 4

FIRST YOU
HAVE TO LOOK

IT WAS A HOT FRIDAY IN JULY, AND MY CLIENT'S ACCOUNTS payable clerk, Linda, told a coworker in the office that she was heading to the affiliate office to drop off payroll checks. After she left, the affiliate's manager arrived at the corporate office to pick up the payroll checks. The corporate accountant said Linda had already headed his way with the payroll checks in hand, but the manager insisted that Linda told him she was going home with a headache and that he would need to come and get the checks. Everyone was confused. Linda's best friend and coworker overhead the two talking, and said, "That's funny. When I went over to Linda's desk to chat with her about our weekend plans, she didn't mention a headache, but she sure was acting funny with the checks on her desk."

The COO, Karen, overheard this and—thinking the best friend's statement was odd—went to Linda's desk and sat down. She opened drawers and didn't find anything amiss.

She noticed the large desk calendar and, for no real reason, lifted it up. Underneath it was a check for $2,200, made out to American Express.

Karen asked herself the obvious question: *Why would Linda, the accounts payable clerk, be hiding a check under her calendar?* There was a credit card number written on the memo line of the check. Karen called me and asked for my thoughts on the matter. Though it was a red flag, there was nothing conclusive. I recommended that she call the credit card company and see if they could confirm whose name was on the account. It could easily have been one of the Company's cards because Karen told me all of the corporate managers carried American Express cards. When Karen called, the credit card company confirmed that the account number did not belong to the company—it belonged to Linda.

When Linda came in on Monday, Karen and the owner, Bill, requested that Linda meet with them. When they placed the check in front of her and asked about it, Linda did what most fraudsters do at first: she denied knowing anything about it. When Karen and Bill explained they had called the credit card company to ask whose account it was, Linda did the second thing many fraudsters will do: she cried and apologized. She fell on her sword and said, "I have taken a little bit of money. Last Christmas I couldn't afford gifts for my kids so I put them on my credit card. When I paid the bills for American Express at work in January, I wrote an

American Express check to pay mine off as well, so my kids could have a Christmas. It just unraveled from there. I've taken maybe thirty or forty thousand dollars, but I promise to pay you back if you don't call the police."

Bill and Karen expressed how disappointed they were in Linda but also expressed that they were thankful she was being honest with them now. After deliberating, they decided to dismiss her from her role and allow her to pay it back, but they knew they needed to quantify the losses between January and July to confirm the correct amount she owed. They realized this would be a large undertaking and, lacking the necessary time and resources, hired me to come in and take a look.

I decided to start looking at the most recent bank statements and work my way back to January. All I had to do was look at the canceled check images and identify checks that weren't company-related checks. Expecting to find only credit card payments, I was surprised to find checks made payable to Linda and other vendors that benefited her—namely her utility and telephone payments. When I finally made it to the January bank statement, when the fraud allegedly started, I had definitive losses of $98,000—a far cry from the $40,000 to which Linda had confessed.

When I told Bill, he was livid—hardly able to believe that this woman whom he had trusted had not only stolen from him but had also lied about it to his face. "Tiffany," he said,

"I want you to go back and find every single check she wrote to herself or her credit card, back to the day she started. When you run out of evidence, you let me know. I want you to find every last dollar she took from me."

Linda had worked for Bill for five years, and she had been stealing from him the entire time. The first check she had written to benefit herself was dated within weeks of her starting employment. The company's total losses equated to $550,000—100 percent of which were checks she had written to herself, her credit card, or other personal vendors.

According to the Association of Certified Fraud Examiners' *2016 Report to the Nations on Occupational Fraud and Abuse*, the most common types of fraud schemes (83.5 percent of all fraud) are asset misappropriation schemes.[ii] These are schemes that involve the theft of cash before it makes it to the bank (theft of cash receipts) or the theft of funds in the bank, withdrawn to the benefit of the employee (fraudulent disbursement schemes). According to the report, losses associated with asset misappropriation schemes average $125,000 by the time they are uncovered. Of the sub-schemes that make up asset misappropriation schemes, the most common is the one Linda perpetrated against Bill and Karen—the fraudulent disbursement scheme, specifically the classification of a check tampering scheme.

---

ii   Ibid., p. 12.

Fraudulent disbursement schemes, especially those classified as check tampering schemes, are the easiest frauds to uncover and quantify. Yet, they are the most common and have the highest median losses (approximately $158,000 by the time they are uncovered).[iii] While some clients call me a "genius" when I find such schemes fairly quickly, the truth is, I am no genius. After years in the field, I simply know how fraud occurs, how it is hidden, and how to find it. You really don't need to be a genius to figure it out. The only difference between me and my clients and their auditors is that I know where to look.

I want you to know what I know. If you know where to look, you will know how to find it.

Even better, if your employees know you're looking, they are a lot less likely to steal. The fact that fraudulent disbursement schemes are so easy to uncover and quantify also make them heartbreaking for the clients involved. They will say, "What's wrong with me that I didn't do something so simple?"

And that simple task? A thorough review of the bank statements and canceled check images each month.

Bill's company initially had some pretty sound systems in place. For one, their CFO reconciled the bank statements

---

iii   Ibid., p. 14 (Figure 7).

each month. But when Linda started, she would sidle up to him and say, "I know you're busy. Let me help you reconcile the bank." It was true—he was busy and thankful for the help. Each month, he would hand her the unopened bank statements and canceled check images. Sure enough, she "helped." She went into the accounting system, cleared all of the canceled checks as part of the normal reconciliation process, changed the payee names from her name to the name of a legitimate vendor, then combed through the bank statements and disposed of the canceled check images attributable to her scheme.

The thing about fraudsters is, they are smart. Sometimes, I find them to be some of the smartest people I've ever met. They know whether or not internal controls are working. They find ways around the internal controls. They find ways to divert someone's attention while they destroy evidence. Linda knew where people were looking and where people were not looking, and she used her sweet disposition and "helpful" nature to continue her scheme.

Understanding fraudulent disbursement schemes is simple. You have money in the bank and your employee needs to figure out a way to get it out of your account so that he or she can benefit from it. Given that fraudulent disbursement schemes are the most common types of schemes we investigate at Acuity and are statistically also the most common, I want to share examples of these schemes and where and how to look for them.

	FRAUDULENT DISBURSEMENT SCHEMES			
RANK	SCHEME	# CASES	% CASES	MEDIAN LOSS
1	Billing	289	27.8%	$ 100,000
2	Expense Reimbursements	164	14.0%	$ 40,000
3	Check Tampering	154	11.4%	$ 158,000
4	Payroll	131	8.5%	$ 90,000
5	Register Disbursements	29	2.7%	$ 30,000

Based on 2,410 total reported cases.

Source: ACFE *Report to the Nations on Occupational Fraud and Abuse*, Figure 7 and 8

The simplest and most cost-effective method for the detection of fraudulent disbursement schemes is to first make sure that the bank statements and canceled check images are returned from the bank every month in paper form. With the advent of online banking, many clients no longer receive the paper form of their bank statements or canceled check images. And most are not logging into the online banking system to conduct a thorough review of individual transactions. Even if they are taking that first step, many are not reviewing all the cancelled check images online. It would take too long to load each and every one of those images and most of us do not have the time to do so. However, a thorough review of paper-form bank statements and canceled check images takes most organizations less than one hour per month to complete.

Next, someone who is not the accounts payable clerk, book-keeper, or the person in charge of approving expenses or writing checks should review the bank statements and canceled check images. This review can be performed by a board member, a member of management who does not have check-writing authority, or an internal or external auditor.

If it's a small company and clients don't feel they have the time or resources for this, I tell them, "Send the bank statements to your spouse, business partner, or tax accountant."

> *There is no better internal control over fraudulent disbursement schemes than somebody looking at the bank statements and the canceled checks every single month.*

That person should review the bank statements and identify whether any ATM or electronic transactions do not match your organization's accounting system and/or do not make sense given the type of business you're in. He or she should review the canceled check images to identify any unusual payee names, amounts, or even signatures. Another easy task is to identify the number of payments being made on utilities, phone bills, and credit cards. Most organizations make a single utility, telephone, and credit card payment each month. If multiple payments are made each month, this could signal that an employee is paying your utility bill and his or her own, too.

In the case of the small private school in the last chapter, if somebody had been looking at the bank statements the very first time Barbara went to the ATM and pulled out $500, or the first time she wrote a check to herself, she would have been caught immediately. If someone other than Linda reconciled the bank statements each month, the checks she wrote to herself and her personal credit card would have been caught.

Expense Reimbursement Schemes

In Chapter 2, we discussed the significant $1 million expense reimbursement scheme perpetrated by Deborah. This was not the only expense reimbursement scheme I've investigated involving millions of dollars. In another case, I assisted in the investigation of three executives of a publicly traded company who were accused by their company of perpetrating expense reimbursement fraud. The fact is, expense reimbursements are one of my first go-to requests for documents when conducting a fraud investigation. It is common to see multiple schemes going on at the same time, and it's quite easy for an unscrupulous employee to remit fraudulent expenses.

Why?

Let's face it. How many of us owners and managers have time to comb through every receipt for every employee who works for us to verify that the receipt on the expense reimbursement form is attached and that the itemized charges are legitimate business expenses?

The problem is, fraudsters know that. They observe whether or not management reviews the reimbursement forms, asks questions, or seeks additional information.

Fraudulent expense reimbursement red flags include:

- Receipts are often missing

- Reimbursement forms are accompanied by receipts showing that expenses are personal (i.e., the fraud is "hidden in plain sight")

- Travel receipts do not match employees' calendars

- Receipts are handwritten (e.g., taxi fare)

- Personal expenses are disguised as business (e.g., spa services at a hotel)

- Signatures on reimbursement forms are forged

- Receipts are turned in one month and the next month the credit card statement is turned in as "proof" of expense—effectively reimbursing the employee twice for a single expense

- Lower level employees know about the questionable expenses but are afraid to say something because they think the boss has "special privileges"

All expense reimbursements should be reviewed when they are submitted. Itemized receipts, and not credit card statements, should be required. The business purpose of the expense and any accompanying person should be noted on the receipt or the expense form, and any travel should match the calendar of the employee claiming the expense.

Billing Schemes
According to the Association of Certified Fraud Examiners, billing schemes are defined as those schemes in which the

fraudster manipulates the organization's purchasing and accounts payable function to generate a fraudulent payment.

The most common schemes I see are personal purchases with company funds and shell-company schemes.

Take, for example, our client, a non-profit foundation. One afternoon, the new administrative assistant to the foundation's executive director found herself with not enough to do in the day, so she took it upon herself to open the mail and see if there were any tasks she could take care of for her boss. When she unwittingly opened a credit card statement, she was so embarrassed. On it were charges for Victoria's Secret, Old Navy, and Macy's, among others. The assistant set the statement aside and turned her attention back to the rest of the mail, thinking that she had inadvertently opened her boss's personal mail. But something about that statement nagged her. She returned to it and reviewed the addressee information; sure enough, it was addressed to the foundation, not the executive director, personally.

The executive director had recently been elected the president of a local business club and was known within the community as a young, up-and-coming leader. She was well liked, respected, and had done amazing work raising money and awareness for the foundation. Given this woman's role in the community, the assistant didn't think what she was seeing was real and that there had to be another explanation, so she set the statement aside again, went home, and thought about it. She couldn't eat dinner and didn't sleep well that night. The next day, all was normal and cheerful at the office, and she was sure that what she had seen on that credit card statement had a reasonable explanation.

When the director left for the day, the assistant opened up the accounting system and found multiple checks that had been written to the credit card for previous payments. The payments were recorded as "office supplies" and "event expenses." She sought out the Bills Paid file to find additional credit card statements so she could compare them to the statement she was seeing.

Oddly, there were no credit card statements among the rest of the paid bills in the file, so the assistant took the statement out again and looked at the thousands of dollars in charges for shopping. There were no fund-raising events taking place at that time (and certainly, they didn't offer items from Victoria's Secret or Old Navy in any of their auction items). She slipped the credit card statement into her purse and took it home with her.

That evening, she called the foundation board president. When they met, they reviewed the charges on the statement and both attempted to rationalize how what they were seeing could be legitimate. They realized, though, that their rationalizations did not hold water.

When the foundation called my firm to comb through

the statements, our findings could only be described as astounding. You could see from the statements that she was regularly shopping, taking personal trips, and even being credited for donating personal funds to the organization, when in reality those funds had come from the foundation's own credit card. Because she was the director and the staffing within the foundation constituted of only herself and the assistant, she could ensure that the mail was always routed to her. When the statements came into the office, she wrote and signed checks to the credit card company using the foundation's checking account. She also created the monthly financial reports and ensured that detailed levels of spending were never shown.

No board member ever asked to look at bank statements or canceled checks. Had they done that, they would have seen thousands of dollars a month in payments to their credit card. If anybody had asked for the actual credit card statements—something so simple—they would have found the charges to Victoria's Secret and Old Navy and all kinds of other vendors, from Amazon to Netflix. None of the charges had anything to do with the business of running a foundation.

Similar to a review of bank statements, if an organization has issued credit cards to staff, then a review of those credit card statements should be performed every month to ascertain whether or not the charges are legitimate business expenses. Those statements should be accompanied by original receipts. As simple as this sounds, it is heartbreaking to see that the majority of my clients didn't recognize the value in taking the time to review source documents like bank and credit card statements until after a fraud is discovered.

It is important to note that I do not blame board members or business owners for their lack of review of source documents. Nor do I blame management of organizations. My goal is to educate. The truth is, there is not enough education related to the subject of occupational fraud or fraud risk. Board members, owners, and managers are busy people who trust their employees to perform their jobs at the highest level. Fraudsters count on this. Using their affable and kind nature, coupled with the knowledge of the fact that management isn't looking at basic documents, they are able to find loopholes in the system. The biggest, and most common, loophole I see is the lack of review of bank and credit card statements.

In the billing scheme category, another common fraud is the shell company scheme. Effectively, an employee creates a "shell company," a fictitious organization with no physical presence and that generates no real economic value. The value in perpetrating a shell company scheme is that a review of bank statements or canceled check images would not easily reveal who is benefiting from the payment (i.e., the employee can avoid writing the check to herself, thus avoiding swift detection).

In one instance, I was called by a car dealer in Seattle who reported that their cash flow just wasn't what it used to be.

Despite selling more cars than they had during the recession, their cash flow had not recovered. Something "just wasn't right."

The dealership hired experienced management, and it was quickly discovered that there were a multitude of accounting "errors." Management was in a bit of a pickle. Mary Beth, the dealership's current accountant and office manager, was the root of the problem. Trouble was, she was a much-loved "member of the family." She had worked at the dealership for more than 30 years and was considered the "surrogate mom" for owners and staff alike.

As the new management dived into the accounting errors, they discovered that Mary Beth had been using the company credit card to take personal vacations. What's more, they found multiple unexplained checks written to Mary Beth that did not correspond to her payroll. Reluctantly, the owners terminated Mary Beth's employment. I was called in to investigate the incidents and to verify whether any other losses had occurred.

A background search on Mary Beth turned up the fact that she was the owner of a business. The name of her business? McBeth Corporation. While the name was not terribly creative, her scheme was terribly effective. A search of the dealership's vendor history uncovered more than $90,000 in payments to this vendor. The payments had been coded to the accounting system in a myriad of ways, most notably as "professional services."

My clients were devastated. Between the shell company scheme, the fraudulent check-writing scheme, and the credit card disbursement scheme, they suffered losses in excess of $325,000, all at the hands of a woman who worked there for 30 years and was affectionately known as the mom of the dealership.

Over the years, I have investigated more than a dozen shell company schemes. There are hallmarks to this type of fraud, which include:

- Payments to the shell company are even-dollar amounts

- Invoices paid by my clients to the shell company are in sequence (i.e., it does not appear that the shell company has any customers other than my clients)

- Invoices are often paid more quickly than normal invoices processed through accounts payable

- Payments are for "services," rather than goods

- Addresses, phone numbers, and/or tax identification numbers for the shell company match the address, phone number, or tax identification number of an employee

- Payments may start small but escalate over time

In order to deposit money made payable to a company, a bank will require that company to have a bank account (i.e., an individual cannot typically deposit funds made payable to a company into his or her personal bank account). In order to open a business banking account, one must typically show the bank the business registration documents for the state the company is located in. As such, the shell must register with the business registry and/or secretary of state's office in order to simply open a bank account. Most states have their business registry documents online and ownership information can be discovered by simply searching on the company name. Conversely, an individual's name can be used as the search term in business registry/secretary of state databases and any corresponding businesses associated with that individual will be turned up during that search.

Payroll

As you may have already realized, many times one fraud scheme is uncovered, but the resulting investigation uncovers additional schemes. Payroll schemes are often one of the first ways a fraud is uncovered. Someone pays herself more money than management or ownership has agreed to. Some fraudsters may give themselves more hours or a higher rate of pay. Others, in charge of the payroll process, may even forgo having any taxes taken out of their checks. The length of time these schemes go on usually corresponds with whether or not someone is double-checking if what was approved for payroll is what is being paid. Think of my client, the doctor, from this book's introduction. The initial payroll scheme had actually gone on for several years. He had approved payroll and Judy had called it in. Judy called in more hours for herself than he had approved. But knowing that the payroll reports were returned to her and not the doctor by the outside payroll service, she knew her scheme would not be caught. Reviewing payroll reports and/or payroll checks after they have been processed is key to identifying the existence of a payroll fraud scheme.

Another form of payroll scheme that we see regularly is called a "ghost employee scheme." The ghost is either a former employee or a fake person created within the payroll system. In most cases, it is the former. Once the real employee leaves the organization, the fraudster continues to issue payroll checks to this individual in perpetuity and routes these checks (or direct deposits) to himself.

Recently, we have investigated two ghost employee schemes, involving large companies with offsite operations. The schemes were quite similar. Each week, the supervisor tallied the time cards and called in the hours for everyone who worked at the offsite location. The corporate office then issued the payroll checks and sent them back to that same supervisor, who passed them out to the workers. It is a perfect recipe for fraud: the same person who tallies hours and calls them in is the same person who hands payroll checks to workers.

By chance, a new manager was hired at one of the sites, and he decided that he wanted to personally pass out the checks that week so he could meet his workers. The supervisor said, "No, I'll do it," but the new manager insisted. By the time the manager had met with everyone and given them their checks, he was left with a mysterious pile of 12 unclaimed checks. That same afternoon, the supervisor quit and was quickly moving out of the house he resided in at the offsite location. The large number of unclaimed checks and the swift move-out of the supervisor were highly suspicious, and my client started to look at the previous canceled checks for these "leftover" employees, inspecting the front and the back. They realized that all of the checks in question were being deposited in the same account over and over again. If two people at the same company were married, it might make sense that their payroll checks were being deposited to the same account. But there should never be 12 payroll checks going into a single bank account in one day.

This particular ghost employee scheme was easy to uncover. And had my clients implemented a few simple controls at the outset, it could have been prevented. First, ensure that the person approving and sending in payroll hours is not the same person issuing the checks to employees.

Second, due to the number of unclaimed checks, a review of the endorsement side (i.e., back) of the canceled checks identified a single bank account was benefiting from the funds. Similarly, if your organization uses a direct deposit system, make sure that deposits to bank accounts are not in excess of one or two individuals per pay period.

Last, analytics related to this offsite location revealed that payroll expenses were grossly in excess, compared to their other offsite locations.

Don't let your organization be a victim of a fraudulent disbursement scheme. The key to avoiding being a victim of the most common fraud scheme is proper review and oversight. In other words, there are simple places to look to ensure that such schemes are not being perpetrated in your organization. Bank statements, canceled check images, credit card statements, expense receipts, and reviews of payroll reports are the best and cheapest fraud detection tools in your tool belt.

Take it from me, you don't have to be a genius!

CHAPTER 4 NOTES

Fraudulent disbursement schemes are the most common types of fraud schemes in terms of frequency. The losses are also typically in excess of $100,000 by the time they are discovered.

Fraudulent disbursement schemes are also the easiest to detect because they leave a trail, typically in your organization's bank or credit card accounts.

The easiest and most cost-effective way to detect a fraudulent disbursement scheme is to ensure a proper review of the bank statements, canceled checks, credit card statements, payroll reports, and expense reimbursement receipts.

Chapter 5

SHOW ME THE
MONEY

"Ms. Couch, my name is Jerri and I saw you in the newspaper last week. I believe you're just the kind of lady we need." I chuckled. "Well, exactly what kind of lady are you looking for?" I replied. Jerri went on to explain.

"Well, my husband and I have owned a business for more than 40 years and now our son and his wife run it. We had a woman steal half a million dollars from us. Our insurance has paid us some of the money back, but the police and district attorney won't prosecute. We've given them the documents and they've even conducted interviews but still nothing. It's been almost three years since we found it out, and they are just sitting on it. I saw you in the newspaper last week and can see you're some kind of investigative accountant. I think that's what we need. I think if we showed you what happened, then you can explain it to the police. Then maybe they'll finally do something about it!"

I told Jerri how sorry I was that they had suffered such a significant loss and could understand that waiting nearly three years must be frustrating. I offered to set an appointment and come over. She told me, "Wait until you see what we have done. My daughter-in-law, our former controller and I will have everything waiting for you."

As someone who has dealt with litigation for more than 10 years, I have seen my fair share of "war rooms" in many a law office. Piles of paper strewn about, binders of important documents, food, and its accompanying trash around the room. When you're preparing for trial (i.e., "war"), this is to be expected.

When I arrived at my client's location and was shown to an attic conference room, I found Jerri, who was in her 70s, and two other middle-age ladies waiting for me in what can only be described as a "war room." There were documents strewn about, the walls were lined with binders of documents, and yes, I even found evidence that they had been eating fast food and other snacks while they worked. These women were clearly prepared for me. They had also clearly spent days in this room and appeared tired and a bit beleaguered. I thought to myself that I should have brought these ladies a bottle of wine!

The women—Jerri; her daughter-in-law, Christine; and their former controller, Bev—explained that they had spent the last few days preparing for our meeting. They had re-created the documents that they had provided to the police and were hoping that I could take a look at everything and explain why the police weren't doing anything to prosecute the woman they claimed had stolen from them.

I asked them to take me back to the beginning and tell me the story of what happened. They described the day, back in 2010, when their banker had called to request several documents for the annual line of credit renewal. As is standard, one of those documents was the accounts receivable aging report, showing amounts customers owed their business. Bev received the call, printed out the requested documents, and sent them right over. Shortly after transmitting the documents, the banker called back. He asked Bev to explain to him who customer "99999-Cash" was and why the balance for this customer was in excess of $300,000? Bev was caught off guard. First, it wouldn't make sense that a "cash" customer would be on an accounts receivable aging because cash customers pay up front and there would be no balance owing. Second, a $300,000 balance for any customer was excessive for the type of business they were in. It simply didn't make sense. Last, why was this customer account seemingly buried in the middle of the aging report? In order to get to the bottom of it, she went straight to the accounts receivable clerk, Lynn.

Lynn, a young woman not yet 30, who had been employed by my client since she was a teenager, burst into tears when Bev started asking questions. She told Bev, "I have really screwed up and made some errors in my postings." She went on to tell Bev that she had gotten behind in her accounts receivable postings and had also made errors. When she went back to fix them later, she was unable to. Without any further questioning or prompting, she told Bev that she had not stolen any money and that she would work with them to figure out the problem.

The next day, Jerri, who had long since retired, was called in to help get to the bottom of the situation. She had set up the accounts receivable system and was best suited to conduct the massive reconciliation effort that was going to be necessary. It was during this reconciliation process that Jerri and Bev discovered several cash receipts registers missing. Cash receipts registers were printed daily and showed the reconciliation of the cash, checks, and credit cards receipted by the offsite stores to the posting of those funds to appropriate customer accounts. In addition to the cash receipts registers, other pertinent documents were found to be missing, making the task of reconciling the accounts nearly impossible. Lynn had been reassigned to cover the front desk and phones while the reconciliation process was taking place. However, Bev and Jerri discovered that Lynn had logged into the accounts receivable module and had made several large adjustments to various customer accounts after being instructed not to log into the system. Their reconciliation process had also uncovered another issue: customer payments were not being applied to the correct accounts. In other words, if customer A made a payment, that payment would sometimes be applied correctly. Other times, customer A's payment would be applied to customer C.

Between the unauthorized adjustments, the incorrect posting of customer payments, and the number of missing documents, Jerri, Bev, and Jerri's son (the current owner) confronted Lynn. She admitted that the "posting problems" had been going on for nearly five years, and she had not told anyone about it because she was embarrassed and overwhelmed. Lynn handed in her resignation letter and even provided Bev a list of "accounts that should be checked," indicating that payments may have been received and not applied or applied incorrectly.

Bev, Jerri, and Christine started the unenviable task of unraveling the incorrectly posted payments. Lucky for them, each store tracked incoming funds by cash, check, and credit card with the identification of the source of funds for each transaction. The ladies confirmed that payments were not being applied correctly; in fact, it seemed, as Bev put it, "she was robbing Peter to pay Paul."

The correct term is a "lapping scheme." In a lapping scheme a customer payment is initially stolen, leaving that customer's account with an open balance. We will call this person customer A. When customer B comes in, his payment is applied to customer A's account. Now, customer A's account is "made whole," but customer B has an open balance. If customer C comes in and his money is stolen, it can set off a "new" lapping scheme, requiring the coverage of customer C's account with a subsequent customer's funds. As you can imagine, this is a nightmare for any business to unravel.

Upon telling me this backstory, the ladies proudly showed me the binders they had put together for me, proving the lapping scheme. The binders showed the manipulation of account after account after account, where funds had come in from certain customers but had been applied to the wrong customer's account. What's more, they showed me that the "99999-Cash" customer account was where Lynn had been tracking her "thefts." At least, this is what they believed.

They told me that they had done all of this work, unraveled all of the payments going back five years, and they believed that Lynn had stolen "close to $500,000."

I looked through the binder. I looked around the war room at the sheer number of documents that had been retained. And I looked at these dear, sweet ladies. Clearly tired. Frustrated. And looking at me with hope. And at that moment in time I had bad news.

I explained that I was sorry that this had happened to them. I told them that it was remarkable what they had uncovered, reconciled, and adjusted on their own. And then I told them that I had a hunch as to why the police had not prosecuted the case. As gently as possible, I explained that with all of the work they had done, they had only proven they had a big accounting mess. I told them that I believed them that Lynn had taken money, but this mess only showed her ability to cover up the losses, assuming there were any. They had not proven that money was stolen. Understandably, they balked. They got teary-eyed. And they exclaimed, "Are you telling us that all of this work was for nothing? That she will just get away with this?"

I looked around the war room. They clearly had decades of documents still on hand. Perhaps hope was not yet lost. I said, "Prove to me that Lynn stole the cash from the stores. Show me how she did that. Never mind what she did to cover it up." They looked at each other. They were skeptical of me, I'm sure, but Jerri decided to humor me.

"Well, I can show you, for the last 40 years, how much cash, checks, and credit card payments have been collected by each of our stores. We have the 'Daily Counter Sales' reports in these binders right here."

"Great," I said. "Prove to me that the guys at the store didn't steal the money before Lynn handled it."

Growing a little agitated with me, she went on. "Well, at the end of the day the guys have to balance their cash, checks, and credit cards to the Daily Counter Sales report and put their initials on it. Then they send a copy of that report and the cash, checks, and credit card slips to the corporate office—specifically, to Lynn. Now, if the men at the stores were stealing the money, then Lynn would have known and would have said something about it because she couldn't have balanced. She never said a word to anyone about cash missing at the stores."

"Excellent," I said. "This is a great start. I'm assuming you have all of your bank statements for the time that Lynn has worked for you?"

Of course they did. This company had retained 40 years of business records.

"Ladies, I think you might be the luckiest clients I've ever met. Based on the documents you have here in these binders along the wall, you can prove how much cash and checks came into your store. You can prove, based on the daily sign-offs, that the store managers had reconciled the funds to the Daily Counter Sales reports. You can prove, based on known processes, that those reports and the funds were directed to Lynn whose job it was to post the payments and prepare the funds for deposit. And you can prove how much money made it to the bank. It's that simple. We need only to prove how much money came in and how much made it to the bank. If there's a difference, we can attribute that to a loss from the theft of cash receipts."

To say these ladies were disappointed was an understatement. What I was explaining to them would be a reconciliation of cash received to cash deposited spanning a five-year period, six business days a week. I was asking them to start all over again and undertake an enormous document-intensive task. Undaunted, they agreed.

Theft of cash receipts is classified by the Association of Certified Fraud Examiners (ACFE) as an asset misappropriation scheme. Cash receipt theft can be classified into two categories: cash larceny and cash skimming.

In a cash larceny scheme, the cash has been receipted on the books of the victim organization. Due to this fact, we call cash larceny an "on-book" fraud. Take a coffee shop as an example. You and I go into the coffee shop today, we order a sugar-free vanilla latte, and give the cashier $5 for our order. The cashier rings up the sale, places our money in the cash register, writes our order on the cup, and we walk out the door with our latte. The money has effectively been recorded as a sale by the coffee shop. At the end of the shift, the cashier may realize she's short paying rent that month or she needs a new pair of shoes. Whatever the reason, if the cashier takes money from the register and places it in her purse before that money makes it to the bank, she has committed a cash larceny theft of cash scheme.

In a cash skimming scheme, the cash is still stolen before it makes it to the bank. However, it is also stolen before it has been recorded as s sale. Due to this fact, cash skimming is considered an "off-book" fraud. Using the same example, you and I go to the coffee shop today, we order a sugar-free vanilla latte, and give the cashier $5 for our order. The cashier writes our order on the cup , and we still walk out the door with our latte. However, she never rings up our order in the cash register. Instead, our $5 gets placed in her apron.

According to the ACFE's *2016 Report to the Nations on Occupational Fraud and Abuse*, average theft of cash schemes is in excess of $50,000 before they are discovered.[iv]

Lynn was not your average cash thief. Her theft scheme resulted in losses to my client of $465,000. While these losses were quite close to the reconciliation process they had completed, it wasn't the accounting mess that proved the loss. In fact, our very simple method of proving the loss by showing money receipted by the stores, as compared to money deposited to the bank, resulted in Lynn's arrest less than one week after we issued our report. Her manipulation of the accounts (i.e., the lapping scheme) only helped prove her intent to cover up the theft. The intentional manipulation of customer accounts was Lynn's undoing, as it was further proof that the employees at the store were not the culprits.

---

iv Ibid., p. 14 (Figure 7).

There is a misconception that cash theft schemes cannot be proven. As a forensic accountant who has successfully investigated cash theft schemes, I disagree. Clients typically have information that will assist in proving thefts from cash receipts.

Most companies have mechanisms in place to track revenue and incoming cash: creating invoices, providing handwritten receipts, making appointments on a calendar, or using a cash register and a point-of-sale system. Customers who sell products will have costs associated with the sale, typically the cost to purchase the items, or something we accountants call Cost of Goods Sold. If cash theft is taking place, a company's sales may show as stagnant, but the cost of goods sold will grow and the ratio between the two figures will no longer be aligned, indicating a potential cash skimming scheme.

The most effective methods for uncovering cash theft schemes involve simply identifying whether receipts exist, quantifying those receipts, and comparing them to the bank deposit records. Surveillance cameras on cash registers can identify sales being transacted but not recorded. Regularly reviewing credits or write-offs of customer accounts can also uncover cash skimming schemes.

In the span of a decade, we have been confronted with numerous cash theft situations, each unique, and each with its own nuances in terms of the types of documents we needed to calculate the losses. I was able to prove that a priest was stealing baptismal fees because the baptismal applications did not match the baptismal-related deposits. We confirmed with parishioners that they had given the priest their application fees directly. We successfully proved losses of cash from a basketball league concession stand by showing that no cash had been deposited during the season and the cost of goods sold percentage for concessions in that year was nearly 100 percent. In the three years prior to the loss, cost of goods sold had remained at the 50-percent level. We have investigated countless thefts at physicians' and dentists' offices where their patient management systems showed receipts of cash, but the bank deposits showed zero cash deposited; or their systems showed credits and discounts that could not be explained by known insurance-related adjustments.

In the case of the small private school in Chapter 3, its main source of revenue was tuition. The expected revenue of the school could have been easily determined by calculating the number of kids attending multiplied by the cost of annual tuition. For example, if you have 100 kids with a tuition cost of $1 per student, the expected revenue would be $100. Comparing that calculation to the actual deposits in the bank accounts would have revealed any significant discrepancies. However, nobody at the private school had done that simple calculation to figure out if the deposits going into their bank were reasonably tied to tuition. Not even the CPA who sat on the board thought to work out the math. If someone had done such a simple calculation as compared to the financial reports or bank deposits, he would have recognized immediately that the school was missing a lot of tuition money. What's more, he would have recognized that other money—fund-raising, lunch money, field trip fees—was also missing.

Do you or your client have a cash business? For the coastal Oregon town mentioned in Chapter 3 and the private school mentioned above, opening up the deposit slip booklets to identify whether currency and coin were being deposited as expected was the first and most simple step toward determining whether a problem existed. Because those deposits slip books indicated no cash was being deposited, in the face of a heavy-cash business, we identified the source data necessary (e.g., receipt books, QuickBooks receipts, etc.) to prove that cash was indeed received but not deposited.

I have found that one of the keys to uncovering fraud is following through on my hunches. I have also found that my clients have hunches long before they even think to call me. Think about my doctor client from the book's introduction. On a gut level, he knew he was seeing more patients, but he was taking home less money. He couldn't quite put his finger on it, but he knew things weren't as they should have been.

Following your hunches, identifying the ways your company's revenue is realized in the form of cash receipts, and identifying the source documents necessary to prove your money is making it to the bank will equate to more money in your pocket that is not lining someone else's.

CHAPTER 5 NOTES

Cash theft schemes are those schemes in which funds are diverted for the benefit of the fraudster before they have the opportunity to be deposited to the bank account.

Cash theft schemes average in excess of $50,000 before they are discovered.

Comparing source documents, like receipts, to actual bank deposits can uncover cash theft schemes. Other clues, including unusual customer credits or write-offs and increasing costs of goods sold as compared to sales, can be red flags of cash skimming schemes.

Chapter 6

WHY AUDITORS DON'T
FIND FRAUD

THE WINTER OF 2009 WAS PARTICULARLY SLOW, AND BY
March of that year I began to consider closing my firm
and working elsewhere. I had a lot of time on my hands,
which suddenly seemed fortuitous when a former client of
mine called. Clark was the CFO for a large company in California, and one of their Washington business sites had an
issue he wanted me to take a look at. Kevin was the controller
at this particular site, which was set to be closed. Part of the
winding down of that company required an asset appraisal.
That appraisal had come in late and needed to get to the
auditors quickly so that the annual audit could be wrapped
up. The appraiser sent a quick email, stating the asset value
in the body of that email, to both Clark and Kevin. Each for-
warded the e-mail to the auditors. However, Kevin changed
the appraisal value of the assets before sending the e-mail
on. The auditor caught the discrepancy and now the audit
was on hold and Kevin was on administrative leave pending

investigation into this discrepancy. Clark said, "I have no idea why he would do such a thing, and we are hopeful this is just some sort of misunderstanding."

I asked him about the company—a manufacturing facility in central Washington—about Kevin, and about the status of the audit. Clark said the audit was done. "The auditors were ready to publish when they found this issue during their quality control process." As for Kevin, he was well respected by the corporate office in California and by his peers. In addition to being the controller of this particular business site, he had also been named the CFO of the company's fastest growing subsidiary, a construction company in Spokane.

We agreed that I would head to central Washington on Monday to investigate the appraisal issue, and Clark would fly up from California and meet me in Spokane on Wednesday to discuss the issue and next steps.

Before hanging up, Clark added, "By the way, if you get to Spokane early, can you inquire as to why we don't have their January and February monthly financials? They are late providing those to corporate. Also, I will send you the draft audited financials to review before you head up there."

Happy to have work to do, I spent the weekend reviewing financial statements. On Monday morning, I arrived to a very somber and empty manufacturing facility where I interviewed all remaining employees, combed through the books and records, and reviewed the data provided to the auditors. There I found a clean set of books and source documents that matched to the accounting entries. Given the company was being wound down, the appraisal value change simply did not make sense. I could not definitively explain why Kevin changed the value of those assets in the e-mail—and I still cannot explain it to this day, more than five years later.

Case closed—or so I thought. On Wednesday, I headed to Spokane to meet with Clark, all the while trying to figure out how to say, "I don't know," in the most professional way possible. "I don't know" is the worst answer a forensic accountant can give a client.

When I arrived at the Spokane location, I was greeted by the staff accountant for the subsidiary. She was new, quite shy, and appeared to be at a loss in terms of what to spend her time doing, as her boss, Kevin, was on administrative leave and had not left her much direction. She brought me to Kevin's office, which was neat and tidy. Three large binders sat on the desk, which the accountant said were the monthly financials awaiting approval—the same financials Clark had asked me to inquire about. I asked her why there were three, and she said they were the December, January, and February financials.

"Why are the December financials 'waiting to be approved' when the auditors have completed the annual audit?" I asked.

"I don't know," she said. "Right before Kevin left, he said

that he 'could explain everything.' I don't really know what that means." She quickly made her exit, leaving me alone with the three binders.

Curiosity got the best of me. I opened the binder containing the December financials and went straight to the year-end income statement, which reported $106,000 of net income. I combed through the binder, looking at all the other statements to verify that I wasn't looking at a month-end statement rather than a year-to-date statement. I confirmed that all other documents (e.g., the balance sheet) tied out to a year-to-date income of $106,000.

I fired up my computer to verify my hunch. Sure enough, I was right. The audited financial statement I had been given for this subsidiary, which was "ready to publish," reported a net income of $1.2 million. In other words, my client had a $1.1 million discrepancy between the audited financial statements and the ones that were sitting on the CFO's desk—and then there was the mysterious and vague statement that Kevin "said he could explain everything."

When Clark arrived at the office, I said I had no idea what was going on at the manufacturing plant in central Washington. I could find no reason why Kevin changed the asset value. Everything there seemed fine, I said, but things in Spokane did not. When Clark asked what I meant, I showed him the million-dollar discrepancy between the audited financial statements and the ones on Kevin's desk.

Now the audit was on an extended hold, and Kevin's administrative leave was prolonged pending an investigation into the financial statement discrepancies. Over the course of the next few weeks, I managed to uncover a huge financial statement fraud scheme, whereby the executive management team at the subsidiary in Spokane was creating fake change orders for their construction company. In a construction company, the only way to increase revenue on a contract is to execute a change order. By creating fake change orders, they had increased the company's revenues and bottom line. That equated to large six-figure bonuses for them that year. It also meant they could retain their status as corporate's "golden child" in Spokane. In fact, due to their "success," the management team had recently graced the cover of the internal corporate magazine.

A construction company books revenue by percentage of completion, based on the value of the contract. Typically, revenue will be fixed per the contract price, unless there is a change to the contract, which allows for more work to be done and thus more revenue to be recognized. I found a series of completely fake change orders that had been created to prop up revenues by more than one million dollars. Due to the size of the contracts and the corresponding change orders, the auditors must have reviewed the same documents I was looking at.

It is an understatement to say that my client was upset. He wanted to know why the auditors hadn't figured out what

I had figured out. To say that the auditors were upset would also be an understatement. They didn't want to be wrong, and most importantly, they didn't want to lose a long-standing and lucrative client.

Upon conclusion of my investigation, I had proposed adjustments to their financial statements in excess of $1.5 million, effectively showing that the company had actually suffered net losses during that fiscal year. Clark and I convened a meeting with the managing partner of the accounting firm to determine the impact on the audit and next steps. The partner in charge of the audit started the meeting by insistently pointing out the mistakes in our investigation. "You are wrong," he said. "Ms. Couch, I have a change order right here in front of me for $850,000. This change order matches the financial statements and our lead sheets. I'm just not seeing the problem you're seeing."

"I know that the *amount* of the change order matches the financials," I told him. "But look at the date of the change order."

He rattled it off.

I said, "Do you see a problem with that date?"

"Well, yes, the date is not even for the same fiscal year we are auditing or for the year they're trying to say it applies to."

"That's right," I said. "Look at the job number on that document."

He read out the job number, which was attributable to an entirely different job.

"Look at the bottom of the change order," I said. "It's not even signed."

He became very quiet and acknowledged that they had missed the discrepancies on the change orders.

In his defense, the CPA partner in charge of my client's audit made the same mistakes the staff auditor had made. He found the *number* he was looking for on the alleged source document, matched that number to his audit schedules and the financial statements, and called it good. The auditors hadn't looked at the document in its totality to determine whether the evidence that was being presented to them was sufficient and relevant to the contract (i.e., job) they were auditing against. The date, the job number, the missing signature—all were clues that the document was a forgery.

These clues were missed by both a staff auditor and a partner in charge of a large public accounting firm—someone with more than 20 years' experience. However, these were not bad auditors. In fact, that firm is considered the best of the best. It is my experience that auditors are not typically trained to have an investigative mindset. Sometimes, being so focused on the numbers can give an auditor tunnel vision.

One of the biggest misconceptions in the business world is that financial statement auditors are a company's first line of defense in finding fraud. It is common for me to hear:

- "We have auditors in here every year and they always say our books are clean. So, there's no fraud at our company."
- "Well, we have an audit, and auditors look at everything, so I'm sure we are fine."
- "How can you tell me that a significant fraud has taken place and our auditors never found it?"
- "Something is wrong in my company; I think we need an audit."

Let me be clear: it is not my intention to disparage the auditors of this world. If I had to do it over again, I would wish that I had the investigative experience I have now when I was working as an auditor. I would have approached those engagements in an entirely different way.

I've been an auditor myself and have managed audits of government entities (cities, counties, school districts, etc.), as well as privately held companies in a range of industries. The work auditors do is important, and they are the sentinels of the investors and stakeholders who must make business and investment decisions based on those financial statements.

An external auditor's job is to determine whether the financial statements (usually the balance sheet, the income statement, and the statement of cash flows) are fairly represented and free from material misstatements—misstatements that would skew the judgment of the individual reading and relying on those financial statements. Annual audits are mandatory for publicly traded companies and governmental entities, and many non-profit organizations are subject to annual audit requirements as well. Privately held companies may have annual audit requirements as a result of lending requirements or other investor-related agreements.

There is a myriad of steps an auditor takes in planning and performing his or her financial statement audit. And while one of those steps requires auditors to consider the risk of fraud in the organization (especially those frauds significant enough to misstate the financial statements), statistics show that they are not the ones who typically find fraud. In fact, of the myriad ways fraud is uncovered, financial statement audits rank at the bottom of the list:

INITIAL DETECTION OF OCCUPATIONAL FRAUDS

Source: ACFE 2016 *Report to the Nations on Occupational Fraud and Abuse*, Figure 21, Page 21.

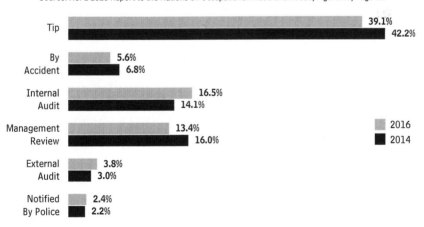

	2016	2014
Tip	39.1%	42.2%
By Accident	5.6%	6.8%
Internal Audit	16.5%	14.1%
Management Review	13.4%	16.0%
External Audit	3.8%	3.0%
Notified By Police	2.4%	2.2%

While the facts show that financial statement auditors are not finding fraud, the same study shows that financial statement audits are the number one anti-fraud control cited by most companies that actually suffered fraud losses:

FREQUENCY OF ANTI FRAUD CONTROLS

Source: ACFE 2016 *Report to the Nations on Occupational Fraud and Abuse*, Figure 47, Page 38.

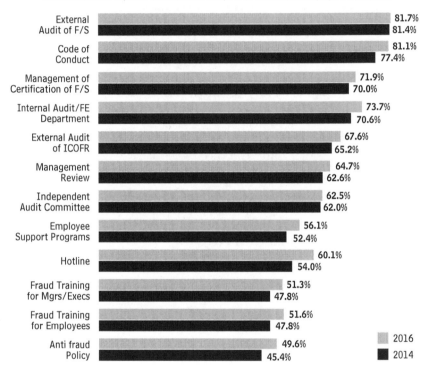

After spending the early part of my career as an auditor and later becoming an investigator who has seen the aftermath of a fraud even after the auditors have given a company a "clean bill of health," I have some theories why the percentage of fraud found by external auditors is so low and also why external audits are the number one anti-fraud control.

The biggest misnomer I hear from clients who call to inquire about our services is their request for "an audit." It is at this moment I need to stop and ask them a simple question. Do you need an audit because your bank or investors or board of directors need an opinion on your financial statements? Or do you need an "audit" because there is something wrong?

Their answer is always that something is wrong.

To Certified Public Accountants, an audit is a very specific type of financial statement engagement, the purpose of which is to provide an opinion on whether the financial statements of an organization are "reasonably stated." To the vast majority of non-accountants, an audit equates to an accountant "looking at everything" and a clean audit opinion equates to "no fraud here, everything is fine."

It is my theory that this misunderstanding of the nature of an audit engagement is one of the main reasons that the number one anti-fraud control in place within victim organizations was their annual audit.

The problem as I see it is, a traditional financial statement audit is simply not designed to find fraud. And while auditors are tasked with understanding fraud risk and assessing the risk that the financial statements will be *materially misstated* as a result of fraud, the very nature of most fraud schemes will not be found during typical audit procedures.

Let's explore some of the reasons why.

My first theory on why auditors don't find fraud is the simple fact that auditors are nice people. In fact, the 2015 Gallup poll on Honesty and Ethics in Professions ranks accountants in the top 10 of professions with high honesty and ethical standards. I have been around large groups of accountants and we do tend to be nice people. We also tend to be "rule followers." We wouldn't steal from anyone, we would return a wallet if we found it in the store, we get up and go to work each day, take care of our clients, take care of our families. Accountants tend to be gentle and kind, leaders in their communities. It is my theory that when you have a worldview like that, it is hard to change your mindset that people who look and act just like you do could be perpetrating a fraud right under your nose.

I had the opportunity to interview Nathan Mueller in December of 2015. Mr. Mueller was convicted of stealing eight million dollars from ING, an international insurance conglomerate. His scheme was quite simple: he wrote insurance refund checks to a fake company that was in his name. He said the annual audits made him nervous, especially in later years as his fraud escalated. He was writing checks to his "company" in excess of $100,000 per transaction, knowing that those dollar amounts increased the risk that they would be flagged by the auditors. To avoid this, he simply created fake documents for them—documents that looked like they came from the accounting system, or invoices that had appropriate approvals but were entirely fabricated.

He told me, "The auditors would ask for the information and I always had the documents ready. They said, 'Thank you very much,' and then went on with their audit. They never tried to prove whether what I was giving them or telling them was wrong. It seemed to me that they were so thankful for the documents. It seemed that they just wanted the documents to get on to the next thing and they were 'just checking a box' or something. It seemed that their job was to believe me, not to try and prove me wrong." Mueller's eight-million-dollar fraud was never uncovered by auditors—a colleague discovered it.

My second theory on why auditors do not find fraud is the nature of audit procedures. They are simply not designed to find fraud. At the beginning of an audit, the auditors will take a look at the financial statements of the company, typically the assets and income figures, and calculate something called materiality. This is the calculated threshold by which if the information (or amount) is withheld or misstated in the financial statements, it would influence the economic decision of the users of the financial statements. As a result of the materiality threshold and components thereof, auditors are forced to look at transactions at or above the materiality level. This is a completely reasonable method of ensuring that financial statements are free from material misstatement; but it simply does not lend itself to finding fraud. That is because fraudulent transactions, by themselves, are not typically at or above the materiality level.

Aaron Beam, former CFO of HealthSouth, in his interview with the ACFE describes how they perpetrated a financial statement fraud at his company. "Bill Owens (former chief accountant for HealthSouth) and I had to explain to Richard [Scrushy, former HealthSouth CEO] that we weren't going to make our Wall Street projections. Richard told us we had to make the numbers. We couldn't let the street [Wall Street] or our investors down. Owens told Richard that he could make entries, entries under $5,000 that the auditors would not look at. [Bill explained] that the auditors had a size or threshold of entries that they looked at. He told us that he could go into the accounting system, create revenue that does not exist, create assets that don't exist, and get the numbers to where they need to be and get us through the audit." Owens did just that, and the next day, Scrushy, Beam, and Owens reported numbers to Wall Street in line with projections. And it was true, the auditors did not catch this fraud either.

Along the lines of the effectiveness of audit procedures, it should be noted that during an audit, auditors do not look at everything. In fact, they take random samples of transactions to test. They test these transactions to verify whether they are recorded in the correct accounts and to verify that internal controls are appropriate, among other things. The chances of a sample selection including a fraudulent transaction among the thousands of transactions available to choose from are infinitely small. Picking a sample is simply not conducive to finding fraud. Such a methodology does not allow for an auditor to easily find a trail of fraud—it's like finding a needle in a haystack. Assuming an auditor does choose a fraudulent transaction to test, the fraudster will likely create roadblocks to a proper review of those transactions by feigning the loss of paperwork or producing fake documents—as in the case of Nathan Mueller. There's simply no time for a skeptical auditor to go digging into mysteries of lost documents.

What's more, fraud doesn't typically look like fraud when it's first found in the accounting records of a company. In fact, most frauds look like regular bookkeeping or accounting errors. One doesn't expect that every transaction will be perfectly recorded in a company's books, as it is reasonable to expect things are recorded in an incorrect account, or that not all revenue was recognized in the correct year. Such mistakes happen because accounting is done by human accountants and humans make mistakes. As long as the number and amount of mistakes does not render the financial statements substantially different than where they should be, then such mistakes are allowed as passes. Auditors are mostly concerned with that threshold of materiality, and as long as the totality of those "passes" doesn't reach that threshold, those errors will likely not be further investigated.

Additionally, most auditors are constrained by budgets and resources. What many outsiders don't know is that in addition to the testing of transactions and understanding of internal controls that auditors are tasked to do, they must also conduct an inordinate amount of due diligence, paperwork, and peer review on their audit procedures. The biggest complaint I hear from auditors is that they are under stress to complete audits on time and on budget so that they can get to the next client engagement. I've had auditors tell me that they've been pushed to "pass" on something they felt wasn't quite right due to time or budget concerns. The limitation of resources means it's easier for auditors to believe what is told to them, or to accept documents as is, rather than pursuing additional information. It's not that auditors are not thorough; with time constraints and budgets in place, auditors can't always be as thorough as they would like to be.

Last, I have a theory that auditors are wearing an invisible scarlet letter A (for auditor) under their suit jackets and they don't even know it. Their status as an auditor creates an invisible wall between them and the people who know something: the whistleblowers. We will explore the role of whistleblowers in Chapter 7. It is my theory that auditors, who perceive themselves as nice people just out doing their job every day, are not actually perceived that way by the people they are auditing. In fact, they are perceived as:

- Scary
- Unapproachable
- Intentionally looking for mistakes or errors (i.e., looking for a "got you" moment)

- People you give the "right" answers to in order to get them to leave as quickly as possible

This dynamic is not realized by most auditors and as a result, they do not make themselves approachable to the very people who have information that a fraud or other significant problem is occurring.

Most fraudsters know that auditors are only looking at dollar amounts over a certain threshold and only take random samples of transactions. The risk of getting caught is really low. They also know that auditors are really nice people. I've interviewed multiple fraudsters who said that when the auditor happened upon a fraudulent transaction and asked for documents representing those transactions, the fraudster would say, "I don't have it," and the auditor would simply pick a new transaction to look at. Auditors give people the benefit of the doubt, rather than assume that the document that can't be found is an anomaly that needs to be looked into further.

When we remember that fraud is a human problem and that fraudsters are some of the most well-liked and respected people in an organization, it is easy to understand why auditors tend to believe what is placed in front of them or what is told to them. Auditors are nice people who wouldn't lie, cheat, or steal. Why would they assume any different of the nice people they are auditing? What's more, their audit procedures are not conducive to finding typical fraud schemes.

Finally, if you or your clients find yourself in a situation where something isn't quite right, I urge you to seek out a trained forensic accountant, not a financial statement audit. Just as if you had a heart problem, you wouldn't go see a dermatologist; or if you needed to update your will, you wouldn't hire a real estate attorney. Accountants have specialties, too. Some accountants are tax experts; others are audit experts. You will find accountants who specialize in business valuation engagements and others who may have expertise in a specific industry (e.g., governmental accounting, aerospace, or manufacturing). Forensic accountants are typically trained accountants who have expertise in understanding fraud schemes, interviewing skills, collection of evidence, writing expert reports that can be held up in a court of law, and testifying skills. Forensic accountants not only look at anomalies, they are also trained to look at a set of accounting or other records and identify what could be missing. A trained and experienced forensic accountant is typically the answer to "something is not quite right here."

CHAPTER 6 NOTES

Traditional financial statement audits are not designed to find fraud, yet the number one anti-fraud control in place in many companies is a financial statement audit.

In fact, less than 4 percent of frauds are found by financial statement auditors.

If you or your client find yourself in a situation where you know or suspect a fraud has occurred, seek out a trained forensic accountant.

Chapter 7

THE QUIET
WHISTLEBLOWER

B EFORE STARTING MY OWN PRACTICE, I WORKED AS A
fraud investigator for a large accounting firm. The firm
was well known in the industry, and when others learned
where I worked, they cooed, "You work there? You must be so
lucky!" I did seem very lucky—a stable job, doing the forensic
accounting work I had long dreamed of doing, with bigger
dreams of one day becoming a partner. Yet what I couldn't
tell people was how my boss would call and harass me at
night, especially after he'd been drinking.

Once, when we were working on a case together, my coworker
asked our boss to bring in an expert for a complicated business valuation that was needed for our damages calculation.
He denied her request, claiming it would cost too much
money, and made her do the valuation herself. A few months
later, she realized she had made a significant error in her calculation. I will never forget the day she called, in a panic, and
we discussed how best to handle it. We agreed that we would
have to disclose the error to the client. People make mistakes,

and it's better to be honest and up-front about it than it is to let someone uncover it when you're on the witness stand or in a deposition. When my coworker told our boss about the error, he screamed at her and asked her why she "didn't hire the expert I told you to hire?" I felt terrible for my coworker. She and I both knew he wouldn't let her hire that expert, and now he was throwing her under the bus. There was little I could do. But for some reason, this situation was the last straw. In hindsight, I wonder why I waited so long and didn't heed the other red flags. His abusive language was intimidating. He wined and dined clients—drinking excessively with them, smoking cigars, and bringing them (and me) to strip clubs. He booked first-class travel to visit us at client sites but often never came to the site at all, while still billing the client for the trip. He sometimes asked us to put administrative costs (i.e., non-billable) on client's bills. He made inappropriate comments about women's appearances. I ignored all of this at first because he was so well liked within the company and landed great clients for the firm. I absolutely loved my job and was excited about the work I was doing and where it might lead me in my professional career. I was also new to the firm and wasn't quite sure how the billing all worked. I'd never witnessed behavior like that as an auditor, and he led me to believe that this was just how fraud investigators acted.

Now, he was mishandling a major client engagement, and my coworker was taking the blame. I was a CPA and a fraud investigator—I had initials beside my name, and all of our reputations were on the line. If I didn't say anything about the mistake, that simple mistake would turn into fraud. And come to think of it, all of these other issues were also hallmarks of fraud, and our names and jobs would be over when it was uncovered. But if I said something, I could lose my job. And I definitely couldn't lose my job—I was the breadwinner in our family, my husband was a stay-at-home dad, and I loved my work. I had big dreams of becoming partner at the firm. If I said something, all of that would be jeopardized. I thought to myself, "Maybe I'm crazy. Maybe I've misunderstood the situation." Then, "Nobody is going to believe me. Everybody loves this guy—he's the rainmaker, the most popular guy in the firm. Everyone wants to work for him."

I'll never forget standing in my garage preparing to leave on the day I was going to blow the whistle. I had made an appointment with the firm's managing partner, but I stood there with the car running and told my husband I wasn't going to go. I tried to go back up the stairs into the house, but he held my shoulders and said, "You're going to go. It's the right thing to do, and it doesn't matter if you and I lose everything. We will be fine. But you can't not say anything."

I met with the managing partner and the HR director. The individuals I spoke with were kind. They thanked me, said they would investigate, and that I could keep my job. "We'll monitor him," they said. When I doubted the effectiveness of that, they suggested that I become an auditor for them in another office. Going to work as an auditor didn't interest me, and going back to work as a fraud investigator under that boss didn't appeal to me either. I thanked them, gave my two weeks' notice, and drove home with the daunting prospect of not having a job in fourteen days.

Not long after that fateful meeting, I started Acuity, my own firm. Several months later, my former employer and former boss parted ways after an inquiry into his actions and behaviors. All in all, this was the best-case scenario: the company investigated an employee's tip, I left voluntarily and was motivated to start my own company, and my former boss was apparently held responsible for his actions.

Unfortunately, when you're in the throes of a situation like this, you can't possibly know how it will turn out. And in my experience talking with whistleblowers, it is my observation that my experience was the exception to the rule.

Whistleblowers are critical to uncovering fraud. In fact, as noted in Chapter 6, the number one way fraud is detected is by a tip. In other words, someone knows something or sees something and says something.

However, the very act of blowing the whistle on a potential fraudster is a true act of courage. When we break it down, we can see why.

First, we have to remember who the fraudsters are. They are typically the individuals whom my clients have trusted the most and liked the best. They are perceived as the last person who would be accused of wrongdoing. As a result, the whistleblower must overcome the fear that the information he or she has will be rejected or not believed. If the fraudster is perceived as well liked and trusted, then the whistleblower is automatically going to assume he or she isn't personally held at the same level of esteem as the fraudster. The fear of rejection is real and is the first reason why many potential whistleblowers choose to remain silent.

Second, whistleblowers having overcome the fear of rejection, must then play out what they may be facing once the information has been shared. Whistleblowers face the fear of being retaliated against by the accused party or their colleagues. They face the fear that their boss will fire them. They face the fear of not finding a job with the same pay or same benefits in a job market that continues to flounder. As they see it, the stakes are high—sometimes too high to actually say something. This is particularly devastating when we consider that 39 percent of fraud schemes are found because someone came forward with information.[v]

One of my clients, a doctor in Tacoma, had a close relationship with his office manager, Diane. When the doctor traveled, Diane house-sat for him. When he and his wife started a family, Diane was there to babysit. She attended Thanksgiving dinner at his house. It was clear to the rest of the staff that she was like family to him.

---

v   Ibid., pp. 26 and 27 (Figure 34).

It was also clear that something at the office was awry. Diane hoarded patient information and yelled at the staff when they offered to help or when they wanted to schedule an appointment for someone. Diane would complain to the doctor that she was overworked, and he would hire an assistant. But those assistants lasted less than a few months, as Diane would find various excuses that the individuals just "weren't working out." The staff noticed that each month she sent out a stack of billing statements, and there was a separate pile she never sent and instead, shredded—a huge red flag for a cash skimming scheme.

The staff brought up these issues with the doctor, but he dismissed them and said they didn't know what they were talking about. After a while, the staff ignored the red flags because they knew the doctor wasn't going to believe them, and even if he did, he cherished this woman too much to follow through and investigate. The staff said, "We figured we might as well not say anything."

The plight of the doctor's staff is a familiar scenario. It's unfortunately common to see whistleblowers shot down or not taken seriously. Countless people come to me with information and say they've spoken up before to no avail. They ask, "What do I do?" And there are usually only three choices: say nothing and keep your job, continue reporting what you've witnessed, or leave and find another place of employment.

Knowing that individuals within your or your client's organization may have information, it is imperative to promote the ability for them to come forward.

A hotline is one of the best methods to allow for individuals to come forward. Hotlines can be implemented in a myriad of ways. There are third-party subscription services, you can have a dedicated phone number and/or website where information can be submitted; or, if you are a small organization and/or you find the subscription services to be cost prohibitive, you can even engage with your outside CPA, lawyer, or board member to handle calls. Inform employees, customers, and vendors of your hotline and encourage them to use it.

As you can see from the ACFE's *2016 Report to the Nations on Occupational Fraud and Abuse* data, there are a myriad of methods whistleblowers are willing to use to inform employers about potential frauds.

FORMAL REPORTING MECHANISM USED BY WHISTLEBLOWERS

Source: ACFE 2016 *Report to the Nations on Occupational Fraud and Abuse*, Figure 35, Page 28.

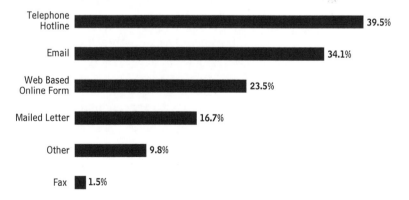

The most important element is advocating for an open-door policy. Customers, employees, and vendors need to feel comfortable enough to call, leave a message, or speak to someone in person. The first step to ensuring this is simple: have a system in place, and make sure that everyone knows where to find it or how to access it.

From there, the key to making your hotline effective is to take every credible report seriously. When management doesn't respond to whistleblowers or brushes them aside, it breeds insecurity in the workplace. Gathering sufficient, relevant evidence to figure out whether or not there is any truth to the allegations is one way to begin, and this may or may not entail hiring someone to help. Of course, you'll probably receive the occasional abuse of the system, with so-and-so calling to complain that so-and-so isn't following the dress code, but those kinds of calls are few and far between.

A common fear of clients is that the hotline will make people uncomfortable or angry—like they aren't trusted. It is my experience that the implementation of these programs often makes the workplace safer, more efficient, and more collaborative. It shows that the business values these voices and opinions and wants to hear them.

If you are an auditor, the best way to get a whistleblower to come forward is to understand how you are perceived by those you are auditing (i.e., the invisible Scarlet Letter A we discussed in Chapter 6) and find ways to dispel the barrier between you and the people you are auditing. None of us realize how scary we are when we walk in the door with "Auditor" next to our name. If you and I were to meet at a networking event or community gathering, we'd likely talk naturally and hit it off. But when I arrive at your office in a business suit, drinking my designer coffee, settle into a conference room like I own the place, start asking questions and requesting documents, I'm suddenly the manifestation of a really scary person. In return, I will find people on their best behavior, the internal controls will always be working perfectly that day, and I will be avoided like the plague. It is just human nature, and we as auditors need to understand it and then find ways to overcome it and become more approachable. While this topic may be the subject of one of my future books, there are simple things you can do to increase your chances that a whistleblower will approach you:

- Fill your coffee cup or eat your lunch in the break room and find opportunities to casually chat with those who are doing the same.

- Never ask if you can interview someone. The term "interview" will strike fear into most people, creating even more of a barrier between you and a potential whistleblower. Let people know you need their "help"; ask whether they have time to "talk to you" about a certain process or procedure you need to learn about. It is human nature to want to help another person.

When you shift your request to "interview" individuals into a call for help, you are automatically breaking down barriers.

- Let people know how to reach you. When a group of auditors are together in a conference room, you are not approachable. If you mix it up and work in an empty office or cubicle, you increase your chances of someone stopping by or chatting with you. If you have a chance to talk to people, give them your business card. Let them know how to reach you, by phone or by e-mail, even after you've completed the onsite work.

These small but effective methods have worked for me in connecting with, and learning from, whistleblowers who perceived that they had no other means to share their information than with me.

Whistleblowers are one of the most important tools an organization has in uncovering fraud schemes, and it is imperative that opportunities for them to come forward are clearly communicated and encouraged. From there, follow-through on those tips is an effective method to ensure future whistleblowers will feel safe to tell you what they know.

CHAPTER 7 NOTES

The number one way fraud is uncovered is through a
whistleblower's tip.

Increase your organization's chances that a whistleblower will
feel safe enough to come forward:

- Open-door policy
- Hotline
- Follow through on reports

If you are an auditor, find ways to be more approachable and
increase your chances of finding fraud during an audit.

PART III

Anatomy of a Fraud...and a Fraudster

Chapter 8

THE FRAUD TRIANGLE

A LOT OF PEOPLE WILL ASK ME, "TIFFANY, WHY DID THIS happen to me?" or "Why do people choose to commit financial crimes when they know they'll be caught?"

Donald Cressey, American sociologist and criminologist, holds the most widely held theory as to why fraud occurs:

Trusted persons become trust violators when they conceive of themselves as having a financial problem which is non-shareable, are aware this problem can be secretly resolved by violation of the position of financial trust, and are able to apply to their own conduct in that situation verbalizations which enable them to adjust their conceptions of themselves as trusted persons with their conceptions of themselves as users of the entrusted funds or property.[vi]

vi   Donald R. Cressey, *Other People's Money* (Montclair, NJ: Patterson Smith, 1973), p. 30.

Dr. Cressey's theory is more commonly referred to as the fraud triangle.

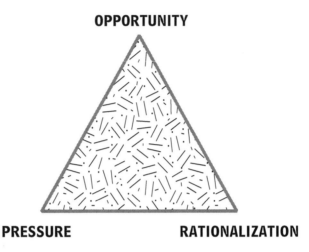

He theorized that three things had to happen for someone to commit fraud. The first was a non-shareable pressure or need, usually something that can't be seen or detected. For instance, a single mom's van breaks down and will need new brakes, but she really can't afford to take it to the shop. Or a spouse was laid off from his job, and the couple can't make an upcoming mortgage payment. It is important, as we are talking about non-shareable problems, to understand the world we live in. It is not uncommon to find that people are living in homes they can't afford, with car payments and credit card debt that can bury them. With little savings or a backup plan, a single event, like a layoff, a few missed days of work, or a car breaking down, can mean the difference between getting by each month or not. While as of this writing, the economy has somewhat recovered, many individuals continue to struggle with the rising costs of food, gas, and medical costs.

What's more, we cannot underestimate the perceived need of individuals to "keep up with the Joneses." The need for grown-ups to "fit in" is an incredible pressure, and I have talked to many fraudsters who started their frauds just so that they could project that they had a certain lifestyle. While they could not afford that lifestyle, they felt that in order to be liked or be with the "in crowd," they needed to act like they could.

Also unique to this issue is the "sandwich generation." With young people choosing to start their families later in life and with aging baby boomers as parents, many are finding themselves placed in the middle (i.e., sandwiched) between caring for their young families and caring for their aging parents. The emotional, financial, and time constraints this places on individuals can be an enormous non-shareable pressure.

One of the most important factors in understanding the nature of internal pressures is to understand that it is non-shareable. Typically, others do not know what someone else's internal pressure is—what's going on in their heads or in their home life. In other words, we cannot control the internal pressures someone may be experiencing.

And those pressures, like life, can change in an instant.

A few years ago, I was called in to perform a fraud investigation at a long-established and family-owned local company. They had recently experienced significant financial difficulties under the management of a close family member. I was asked to come in and determine whether the financial difficulties were a result of fraud. At the same time, the company was working with a turnaround expert to determine whether to continue in business or wind down and close. I was fascinated by this company for various reasons, but primarily due to the tenure of its employees. At the time of my engagement, the company employed approximately 50 people. And the person with the least amount of tenure had worked there 10 years. One woman I met had been there 40 years. To me, this was a remarkable testament to the company and its founders.

Nevertheless, the family decided it did not have the time, financial capacity, or leader who could carry the company through this difficult time, so they chose to shut down the business. I will never forget the day. Everyone came to work on that Tuesday as if it were any other day, but at three o'clock the owners called a meeting in the break room to tell the staff they were going to close for good. A few hours before, they were eating lunch in that same break room, oblivious to the significant change they would be facing before five o'clock that day.

Circumstances can change faster than anyone can ever

anticipate. One morning you come to work and find out you don't have a job to go to the next day. How do you pay rent? A mortgage? How do you plan for retirement? Pressure changes in someone's life doesn't always mean he or she will turn to drastic measures like fraud, but it's critically important to understand the importance of financial pressures when we are discussing the anatomy of a fraud.

The second element is also not apparent: someone's ability to rationalize taking your money. A single mom who needs to get to work might rationalize that she can pay for her broken van's brakes with the company bank account and pay it back before anyone realizes it. The person unable to pay the mortgage might rationalize that you've laid off several people in his department and asked him to take a pay cut; so not only is he doing his job, but he's doing the job of others' too—and he deserves to be compensated appropriately.

Take the case of the volleyball club thief. This was as simple as it gets, in terms of establishing guilt. It was the responsibility of one of the mothers in the girls' volleyball club to take the team money to the bank. However, she had been depositing the funds and then immediately withdrawing money from the account, right there at the teller window. The bank statements clearly showed the deposits and withdrawals; and the withdrawal documents we received from the bank all had her signature. It was a clear-cut case, and all that my client wanted was for her to admit what she had done and to pay the money back. Nevertheless, she would simply not admit to it.

What made matters worse was that she had a critically ill child at home. My own child was the same age as hers, and I remember thinking, *I can't even imagine what it would be like to have a child that sick.* My clients, knowing her situation, did not want her to go to jail. They told me, "Tiffany, we just want you to get a confession out of her. We want you to explain to her that if she tells the truth then we will be as lenient as possible, because nobody needs their mother in jail."

I sat down with her and tried to get her to see reason. I kept telling her, "Listen, we know that this is an uncomfortable situation. The evidence against you is overwhelming. We just want you to admit to it and promise to pay it back so that we can all move on from here." But she would not budge.

Finally, after more prodding, she volunteered, "Well, yes, I did withdraw that money, but I used it to buy volleyball equipment for the team." She insisted that she had spent the money on volleyballs and nets. She swore that she could come up with receipts for all of these purchases.

I informed my clients of this and they said, "Fine. We'll give her another few days."

When she sent me the receipts, I called the stores to verify them—and they all turned out to be forgeries. Now, not only did we have her on theft, but we also had her on forging receipts. All she had done was get herself into bigger trouble.

The club was ready to call the police. And yet, they really wanted to give her any conceivable way out. They asked me to interview her one more time.

"Look," I said, "not very many people in your predicament have an opportunity like they are giving you. They don't want you to go to jail – they just want the truth of what happened."

Still, this did not faze her. I began to wrack my brain. I knew that she had a good job and I knew her spouse also had a good job. Why would she have taken this money?

I hesitated to bring her son into this, but I had to ask. "Was it to buy prescriptions for your son, or for doctors' appointments?" This was a reason that anyone could understand.

"No, no," she said. "My insurance covered all of that."

I thought to myself, *They are going to call the police on this woman, and it's going to be just terrible.* But then, all of a sudden, I had an epiphany. I noticed three things about her all at once. Number one: She was carrying a very expensive Coach purse that I had not noticed the first time around. Number two: I noticed she had fake nails. Number three: She had a tan, and it was January in Washington State; nobody has a tan in January in Washington State unless they're paying for it at the tanning booth.

I looked at her and said, "You just wanted to feel like a regular mom, huh?"

"What do you mean?" she asked.

"Well, the other moms, their kids are healthy and get to go to school every day. Their kids aren't in the hospital. The worst thing that could happen is their kids maybe stay home with a fever. The other moms, they get to have their nails done, they get to go shopping, they get to go to the tanning salon, and you didn't get to do any of that, did you? You had to take care of your son."

The tears came down. "Yes, that's all I wanted! I just wanted to feel like a regular mom. I didn't think I was hurting anybody. Everyone still got to play volleyball."

The problem with rationalization is that it may begin soundly enough, but it can snowball out of control. Before you know it, the brakes have been paid for, the mortgage is current, but the person doesn't stop there. The fraud continues, even when the original reason for it is diminished.

The first two elements of the fraud triangle—internal pressure and rationalization—are interior, unseen elements. We cannot control the pressures an individual is facing, nor can we control their private rationalizations.

That is why it is imperative to understand the one thing any business can control. And that is the third part of the fraud triangle: opportunity.

Opportunity is access to the checkbook or bank account, the cash that comes in each day. Opportunity is having access to the financial side of the business, the ability to take the money and cover it up.

Business owners, managers, and accountants must limit opportunity as much as possible. One of the biggest mistakes I see made is that businesses will implement internal controls on everyone except the person they trust the most, or the person they least suspect. "Trust" becomes the internal control and too often, it turns into my clients' biggest problem.

Opportunity is the only aspect of the fraud triangle that a business can control, and opportunity can be managed in a myriad of ways: proper internal controls, segregation of duties, management oversight on processes, appropriate software controls limiting access to employees, and providing ongoing training.

Safeguards must be put in place around everyone— regardless of who they are or what their role is. Proper internal controls and oversight is the best way to limit the chances of fraud. Take it from my doctor client whom I introduced you to at the beginning of this book:

"I put safeguards around everyone except Judy. I didn't think I needed to. I trusted her the most and I thought she was the exception to the rule."

CHAPTER 8 NOTES

Understanding the fraud triangle is key to understanding the importance of internal controls and proper oversight over all employees, no matter how trusted they are.

Employers cannot control the financial pressures indivdiuals are facing, nor can they control the rationalizations that one might use to start a fraud scheme.

The one thing employers can control is their employees' opportuntiy to steal.

Chapter 9

RED FLAGS ARE FLYING

O NE OF THE FIRST THINGS PEOPLE TELL ME ABOUT THE person I'm investigating is also one of the first red flags most businesses see: the suspect's lifestyle doesn't add up to their known or suspected income sources. When Linda first started working as an accounts payable clerk for Bill, her car was repossessed out of the employee parking lot. Having your car repossessed at your workplace is a significant event and must have been devastating for Linda. It certainly left an impression on her coworkers. Bill graciously loaned Linda money so she could buy a car in order to get to work, and they agreed to deduct funds from her paycheck to repay it. Five years after the repossession, all of the guys in the office told me that Linda was driving a brand-new Audi to work every day—an expensive and luxurious vehicle.

The car wasn't the only suspicious lifestyle item. The ladies in the office told me that Linda never wore the same outfit twice, and that her purse always matched her shoes. They also told me that she drove to the "big city" to get her hair done—spending hours in the car and paying for high-end salon services.

Everyone told me that Linda was a big spender. They indicated that on weekends she would travel out of town to the large shopping malls. Her coworkers commented that Linda's children had toys of all kinds, big and small. They noted that her kids had everything from jet skis and snow skis, to the latest electronic gadgets. The care paid toward her physical appearance and the expensive luxury car and gifts seemed inordinate, given that only five years ago her vehicle was repossessed, and she had borrowed money from her employer to buy a used car to get to work. On top of that, Linda earned fifteen dollars an hour and her husband didn't earn much more. They also had two teenage boys at home. Her lifestyle seemed extravagant, given the circumstances.

As Linda's lifestyle became more extravagant, it appears that she created a "cover" to explain her lavish lifestyle. She told everyone at work that she had become a consultant for a multi-level marketing company, selling "candles." She explained that her newfound fortune was a result of her extraordinary gift at selling candles.

Funny thing was, no one seemed to think she spent much time actually selling candles or having "candle parties" to sell her wares.

Linda is not an anomaly. If we were to comb through the

fraud cases in my filing cabinets, almost all of them would contain instances where people commented—often directly—on the suspect's lifestyle: the expensive cars they drove, the lavish trips, the shopping sprees, the high-end watches. Most of the fraudsters aren't working hard to hide it—many want their affluence to be seen.

Most people know what's going on or have an inkling that something is not quite right. Still, communities are often surprised when I arrive at a company to investigate—incredulous, even, that something could have happened right under their noses. Yet it doesn't take long for that feeling to wear off. As evidence is uncovered, there is a kind of cascading effect, where people relay information they previously ignored. Suddenly, everyone seems to remember something suspicious that they now see as being a sign of something more sinister.

Gift Givers

Remember our fraudster Lynn from Chapter 5? The young woman who perpetrated a large theft of cash scheme against Jerri, Bev, and Christine? The ladies described Lynn as a happy young woman who was a joy to have in the office each day. She, too, however seemed to have a mismatched lifestyle. During her tenure at the company, Lynn married one of the men who worked in the warehouse. As such, it was well known to my clients what the couple's likely combined income was. Nevertheless, I heard stories about Lynn's plastic surgery and expensive Botox treatments, her second home at the beach, and the husband's passion for race car driving.

One of the memories that stuck with each of the ladies was how kind and thoughtful Lynn was with everyone in the office. They described the fact that Lynn remembered everyone's birthdays and gave them personalized, and often, expensive gifts. For one individual in the office, she remembered that one of the local bakeries made a special soup each Wednesday and she'd bring it in, "just because." The most expensive gifts were given to the owners. They would tell her "she shouldn't have" and "you don't need to do this." They asked her to stop, but Lynn couldn't seem to help herself. Jerri, Bev, and Christine remarked that Lynn seemed to love the attention she got when she gave the gifts.

Hardest Workers

Another common "after the fact" theme that I hear is how much the fraudster worked. I will often hear that the fraudster was the first one to work each day and the last one to leave. Fraudsters always retrieved the mail. They rarely took vacations. If vacations were taken, fraudsters would "button up" their desk before leaving to ensure that no one needed to help or assist.

Take the doctor in Tacoma, whose beloved office manager had worked for him for the entirety of the fourteen years he was in business. He could not recall a single instance of her taking a vacation or a day off.

The doctor's beloved office manager was the first one into the office each day and always was the last to leave.

Deborah, the executive who perpetrated the expense reimbursement scheme, was the same. She was known to work tirelessly, over weekends and holidays.

When one thinks rationally about a job, we all know we need breaks. We need weekends off and holiday or vacation time to clear our minds, rejuvenate, and rest. Fraudsters, however, need two things: time and privacy. First, they need time—time to do their job, steal the money, and cover it up. They also need privacy. Going back to my doctor client from the beginning of this book, I was able to prove through the audit trail report that most of the cover up, the manipulation of his books and records, occurred in the early mornings before everyone came in or late at night after everyone left work for the day.

Refuse to Relinquish Control/Train New Employees
Along with being the "hardest working" employees, we will often hear that the fraudster will refuse to relinquish control over his or her job duties. I have encountered several instances of employees who were seemingly overworked, but when offered the chance to offload that work, they found reasons not to accept the help or found reasons to fire the employee charged with helping with the work load.

This red flag can be a difficult one. When presented with an opportunity to talk to an employee who exhibits this behavior, I often ask one simple question. This question is used to decipher whether we have an ego problem or a potential fraud problem.

"If five dollars was missing from this organization, all roads point to you. How do you feel about being in that position?"

People with a big ego will think rationally at this point. I will see the color drain from their face. I will see a look of realization in their eyes. They will put their hands on their face. And they will say, "Oh my gosh, I never thought of it that way. I would be devastated if I were accused of any wrongdoing. I just love my job. I take a lot of pride in it." They are able to see that their pride could get them into a lot of hot water.

Alternatively, potential fraudsters will stall. They will dig in. Even faced with the realization that they could be accused of wrongdoing they will say things like, "How dare you even question my integrity? I swear on my mother's grave that I would never steal a dime from this place!" Fraudsters will do anything and say anything to avoid additional scrutiny or relinquish control over a process or procedure that could reveal their crimes.

Financial Information Is Late and/or Riddled with Errors

It is always curious to me that my clients will tell me how many *years* they have gone without getting any meaningful financial information from those in charge of their finances or accounting. In the case of the small city on the Coast of Oregon, they went more than three years without an audit, with the city clerk stalling with phrases like "I'm too busy."

Barbara at the private school had to be cajoled into providing financial reports to the school board. When she did, they were described as messy, the numbers often didn't add up, or the information "didn't make sense." I was provided an example of a financial report submitted to the school board and I noted right away that the balance sheet didn't balance! No one had noticed this error, not even the CPA who served on the board.

Lynn's accounts receivable posting was riddled with errors.

Tom had not reconciled the bank accounts for a multi-million-dollar company in more than six years.

As someone who has had roles as a bookkeeper, accounting manager, and auditor, I can affirm that accounting is not rocket science. A good bookkeeper or accountant should be able to provide financial reports to owners or management with a click of a button. Take heed when you find yourself in a situation where you can't get basic financial information from a bookkeeper or accountant. This can be a red flag of fraud.

Addictions

During my tenure as an auditor, we were engaged to audit a large county in California. Just before our audit was to begin, we received a curious call from the county administrator. It seemed that their beloved intern, who was poised to soon graduate from the local university and be promoted to a position with serious career potential, had called into work that morning informing them that when they opened the safe, they would find missing funds.

Sure enough, there was more than $10,000 missing from the safe that morning.

It turns out that the intern had a serious gambling habit. Everyone knew that he enjoyed going to the local casinos and that he seemed to have a winning streak. What nobody knew was that he would "borrow" funds from the county's safe each night, returning the borrowings early each morning. He ran into a problem when he lost all of the money the night before. He and a family member accessed the safe in the middle of the night, took more money in hopes of winning it all back, and lost those funds as well.

In a similar case, many years later, I investigated the manager of a local credit union who was stealing cash to play bingo. Everyone knew that she played bingo several nights per week. What they didn't know is that similar to the young intern at the county, she, too, was "borrowing" funds to play bingo.

For the little town in Oregon, there was an initial connection to the city clerk's nightly drinking and playing video poker at the local bar.

Gambling addictions and drug and alcohol addictions can be an outward sign of pressure that could cause an individual to perpetrate a fraud scheme.

The Association of Certified Fraud Examiners tracks the behavioral red flags that are displayed when fraud is uncovered.

BEHAVIORAL RED FLAGS DISPLAYED BY PERPETRATORS

Source: ACFE 2016 *Report to the Nations on Occupational Fraud and Abuse*, Figure 94, Page 68.

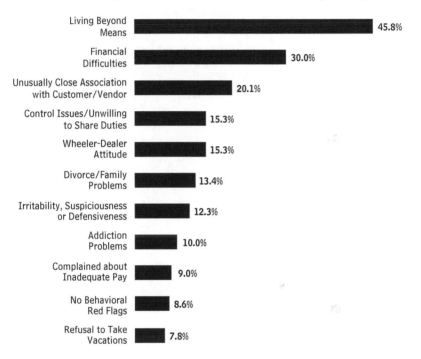

Living Beyond Means	45.8%
Financial Difficulties	30.0%
Unusually Close Association with Customer/Vendor	20.1%
Control Issues/Unwilling to Share Duties	15.3%
Wheeler-Dealer Attitude	15.3%
Divorce/Family Problems	13.4%
Irritability, Suspiciousness or Defensiveness	12.3%
Addiction Problems	10.0%
Complained about Inadequate Pay	9.0%
No Behavioral Red Flags	8.6%
Refusal to Take Vacations	7.8%

It is important to note that behavioral red flags are just that. They are red flags only. Just because an employee exhibits one or more of these red flags does not equate to evidence of fraud. I was presented with an instance where every "red flag" was flying. My client, a doctor new to a practice, had asked for simple financials for the practice and the office manager refused to provide the information. What's more, his business partners became angry at him for insisting on the information.

The doctor and his wife described the situation to me. When I asked about the office manager he told me that she had worked for the practice for more than 30 years. She was the only person to receive patient and insurance payments and post them to the patient accounts. She prepared the funds for deposit and took them to the bank. She paid all of the practice's bills. He had no idea whether or not she signed the checks because he was never allowed to see any. He assumed she reconciled the bank, too. What's more, she wasn't providing any basic financials to him. He was concerned something was amiss.

Truth was, I was concerned, too.

He paid me to unravel the books. I looked at the patient system, verifying that all money received had made it to the bank. I reviewed patient write-offs and credits, noting that they were supported by doctor notes and/or insurance contract adjustments. I reviewed the bank statements and canceled checks and verified that all expenses were supported by invoices. Same went for payroll. Nothing was out of the ordinary there. When I informed the doctor and his wife that for a two-year period of time, I could find nothing, he asked me to keep going. So I did, looking further back in time, I still found no evidence of fraud.

It seemed to me that he had a really trustworthy employee with a really big ego. I could find no evidence of fraud at all.

When it came time to pay my bill the office manager called me under the pretense of needing a "W-9 form."[vii] Once we discussed the nuts and bolts of getting the form over to her, I thanked her. It was clear she wasn't finished with the phone call. She said, "You know, I'm upset by how much the doctors need to pay you. I feel like it's all my fault." I couldn't help myself, I took the bait. "Why do you say that?" I asked. "It's just that it hurt my feelings so much when Dr. Tim asked for the financial information. He asked it in a way that made me feel like he didn't trust me. I just couldn't believe that anyone wouldn't trust me."

I told her that I understood how much that must have hurt her feelings. It would have certainly hurt my feelings. I then pointed out, "You know, if there was $5 missing, the blame will point to you. You are not safe in your job."

The phone got very quiet. And she said, "I never thought of it that way. Oh my gosh, you are absolutely right. It's even worse, though."

---

vii IRS Form W-9, Request for Taxpayer Identification Number. Provided to companies or individuals who are required to file an information return with the IRS for income, rent, or interest paid to you.

"How's that?" I asked.

"If I got hit by a bus, they would be up a creek. I'm not getting any younger and they could not survive without me. We need to change this right away." It is my understanding that they hired additional staff and found ways to improve the internal controls and financial reporting at the practice.

Take notice of red flags of fraud. From lifestyle inconsistencies to too much control over a business function, to addiction and personal problems, to the lack of basic financial reporting—these flags are consistent themes in my case files, and had they been heeded sooner, many frauds would have been uncovered more quickly and my clients would likely have sustained less monetary losses.

CHAPTER 9 NOTES

Certain red flags are commonplace in detecting fraud. Most frequent inlcude:

- Lifestyle of fraudsters does not match their known or supsected sources of income.
- They are gift givers and/or have a "wheeler-dealer" attitude.
- They have known financial difficulties at home.
- Financial information is error-prone, late, and/or non-existent.
- There are known or suspected addiction problems.

Chapter 10

CAUGHT! FRAUDSTERS ACT LIKE YOUR KIDS

SIMILAR TO THE COMMONALITIES OF RED FLAGS REGARD-ing lifestyles, gifts, and lack of financial reporting, I have found that my clients describe commonalities in the behaviors of the fraudsters both prior to when they were caught as well as when the irrefutable evidence is placed in front of them.

The more crimes that I have investigated and/or been aware of, the more solidified I have become in my theory that many of the behaviors displayed by fraudsters are the same my children have displayed to deflect or deter my attentions when they were "up to something." They are the same behaviors my friends and I displayed to our own parents while growing up. It's my theory that we are all just kids in adult bodies!

First, we need to talk about some of the red flags and corresponding behaviors that are often displayed while the fraud is going on, but before anything is suspected. It is important to recognize these behaviors to ensure that you recognize them when you see them. If you find yourself faced with these behaviors, find ways to identify and take custody of documents (like bank statements, sales reports, credit card statements, receipt books, etc.) that can prove or refute what you're being told.

The Plausible Explanation

The most common theme I hear about is the lack of financial reporting or errors in the financial reports provided. My clients will tell me that they questioned things on the financial reports, but they were always given a reasonable explanation and never thought to look into the issues further.

Me: "Why are you in here playing video games? It's the middle of the school week and you know you aren't supposed to be playing games until the weekend."

Kid: "Mom, you don't understand. I'm not actually *playing* my video game. I'm just checking in on my base to make sure my guys don't get killed."

Sound familiar?

As humans—trustworthy humans at that—it is natural that we would want to trust those who are closest to us. Fraudsters know this to be true. They will always have a plausible explanation for anomalies, expecting that their explanations will be taken at face value without any request for source documentation, because they are held in high esteem and are trusted by their employers.

Linda, for example, might have been caught many times over. Bill and Karen and others told me about the dozens of times she was confronted with errors in her work. Most notably, there would be two of the same expense in a single month. As an example, they might see the "legal expense" category for a month and see two line items in that category. Linda would say, "Shucks, I did it again! I accrued this month's and last month's legal billings into a single month. I'm so sorry. I will go back and fix it." Trouble was, no one verified whether there were actually two legal bills in the paid bills file and whether the amounts in the general ledger expense account matched the billings from the law firm. What's more, no one verified whether she had gone back and fixed the error. Had someone double-checked Linda's story, he would have found there was only one legal billing that month. The other "bill' was actually a check she had written to herself. She had gone into the accounting system and changed the name of the payee from her name to the name of a legitimate vendor (like the law firm). Linda's plausible explanations were always at the ready, and she knew that nobody would pull the bills out of the drawer.

How Dare You?
Second, when pressed on issues, fraudsters will often push back using a variety of methods to make the questioner feel bad about himself.

Kid: "Mom, after the homecoming dance, there's going to be an after-party at Mike's house. I'd like to go."

Me: "Will there be any girls there?"

Kid: "Yes, but that's no big deal. They will be leaving by midnight."

Me: "I don't think that's a good idea. It's your first homecoming dance. I think we will ease into these things and say no to the after-party this time around."

Kid: "Mom, are you kidding me? What, you don't trust me? I get good grades, I volunteer, and I'm a good kid. Everyone else is going. This is so lame. It's like you and Dad don't want me to have a life."

Sound familiar?

As a mother of two teenage boys, I'm finding this method to be very effective! And I can attest, they can kick you right where it hurts and get you to second-guess whether or not you're being too harsh. (For the record, he didn't go to the homecoming after-party!)

Fraudsters will do the same. They make their victims feel bad about themselves. Clients describe an almost-paralyzing fear of asking the suspected fraudster any basic accounting or banking-related questions. They don't want to ask too many questions because they're afraid of the reaction they might receive, and they don't want to anger anyone by questioning their work or their loyalty to the organization. They also don't want to look or feel stupid. They might think, *I'm not a numbers person, so I wouldn't even know what I'm looking at anyway.*

I mentioned the basketball league case in Chapter 5. Certain board members had been asking for financial reports and bank statements. The treasurer refused, claiming she was busy or that she "forgot" to bring them to the board meetings. When pressed, she went on the offensive, calling board members who were her friends, claiming that the other board members were being "too hard" on her and "pressuring her" to provide financials. The sympathizers convinced the other board members to back off. They did. They described feeling frustrated not to be able to get basic financials, at the same time struggling with the fact that they did not want to be perceived as individuals who could not get along with the group. It took the election of a new board many months later to get basic financial and bank statements. Once they did, they realized that all of the league's money was gone.

Sometimes the behavior is so astonishing that I am surprised that the behavior itself is not a cause for termination of employment. But then, even I have to remember: the fraudsters are well liked by their employers, are infinitely trusted, and my clients are nice people. Of course they are going to internalize the issue.

Once, a business owner called and said he believed his office manager was stealing from him. When he asked how he should proceed, I told him to send me the company's bank statements and canceled checks. The phone went silent.

"I can't do that," he said.

"Why not?"

"She has all my bank statements and canceled checks in her office."

"Well, just go ask her for them."

"She might get mad at me for questioning her. I don't want her to be mad at me."

"Okay, then go online and get the statements from your banking site."

"Well, I can't do that either because she has all the passwords and she'll know something is wrong if I ask her for the passwords."

"Then why don't you go to the bank? They'll give you your bank statements and canceled checks."

"I don't even know my account number."

"They'll look it up for you. They can do all of that for you."

He never followed up with me, and his CPA later mentioned that he was just too afraid to confront the situation for fear of upsetting the office manager.

I've said it a lot in this book and I will say it again. Fraudsters use their ability to be liked and trusted to gain access and perpetrate fraud. If an employee is unlikable, seems shifty, and is always late to work, an employer is not going to trust her to handle money or run a business or manage an office. This likability allows fraud to go on for a long, long time before fraudsters are caught.

Also, I can hardly believe how smart fraudsters are. They seem to me to be infinitely intelligent, finding ways to maintain their job, often maintaining warm and friendly relationships, all the while perpetuating and hiding fraud. The ways they hide it and get away with it—the lies they tell—are clever and savvy. One has to wonder why they're not utilizing this intelligence to do something good in the world.

I cannot stress enough how unbelievably good they are at maintaining their duplicitous lives.

Similar to the commonalities in their behaviors while the frauds are going on, I have discovered commonalities in what happens once the fraudsters are presented with evidence of their wrongdoing.

- STEP 1 – DENIAL: When a specific issue is uncovered and the accused person is confronted with the evidence, she will first deny knowing anything about the transaction. This denial can be verbal. She may not even look at the paper placed in front of her or she may go so far as to physically push the paper away from her.

  When Linda was caught writing a $2,000 check to her credit card company, she denied knowing anything about it. When Deborah was caught forging her boss's signature, she indicated that she "didn't know how to answer" the CEO's questions.

- STEP 2 – TEARS AND ACKNOWLEDGMENT: When the evidence in front of fraudsters becomes irrefutable, they will turn on the tears. They will acknowledge what has been found and will often exclaim how sorry they are. They may beg for forgiveness.

  When Bill and Karen told Linda they had called and confirmed the account number was hers, there was no way out for Linda. She began to cry and softly said, "You're right, I did it." Clients tell me all the time that when a person confesses he or she cries, and it happens in my own interviews with fraudsters. They turn on the waterworks and launch into a sob story. It is not uncommon, after the fact, to wonder whether this kind of emotional reaction is an attempt at gaining empathy and continuing their need to control the situation.

- STEP 3 – PLEA DEAL AND APOLOGY: I call Step 3 the "Plea Deal" because fraudsters, when faced with irrefutable evidence and a difficult situation they would like to literally run away from, will say things like, "If you don't do anything, I promise to pay it back." "I only took XXX dollars. I'm so sorry."

Linda apologized and explained that she couldn't afford Christmas gifts for her kids, so she put it on a credit card and used the company account to pay it off at first. When she was asked about how much she took, she estimated it was "about $40,000." She apologized profusely, said she'd never do it again, and promised to pay it back.

The confrontation will usually lead from denial, then to the admission of some level of wrongdoing. There will be tears and there will be moments of negotiation. My clients, being nice people who trusted and very much liked the perpetrator, will be relieved about their honesty. They will explain to me that they feel sorry for the fraudster who "made a really poor decision." Too often, many of these clients will accept the admission, make a deal to have the perpetrator pay it back, and call it good. Still something won't sit well with them, and I'm often called to look further and/or write up a report for insurance-related purposes.

When I am presented with this situation, I give my clients a multiplier of three. That's my general rule. If a fraudster admits fairly quickly to a wrongdoing, multiply the number he admitted to by three because typically, that's the amount of fraud losses we will find after the fact. Fraudsters, both men and women, will turn on the tears and say they are sorry. They are in an uncomfortable situation and they will do whatever it takes to get out of that uncomfortable situation, including admitting to some wrongdoing. They will use the phrase, "If you don't escalate this (code for not calling the police), I promise I will pay it back."

In my experience, this scenario is how the fraudster maintains control over the situation. They will fall on their sword, they will cry, they will admit to some of the losses in the hopes that *you won't keep looking*.

Think about it in these terms. If you are a parent, or remembering back to when you were a child, recall a situation where you or your kids were in trouble. Did you typically deny that trouble when it was first presented to you? Yes, I'm pretty sure you did. "I don't know how Mr. Smith's window got broken." Then, when presented with irrefutable facts—"Son, could the broken window have anything to do with the baseball bat in your hand?"—you had no choice. You cried. You told your mom or dad you were sorry. That it was an accident. Sure, you were grounded. You had to fix the window. But it was a lot less trouble than had they found out that you and your friends were actually aiming for Mr. Smith's window, to see who could hit it from the farthest away.

Grown-ups are just kids in adult bodies. When faced with trouble, they react very much the same. Control the situation. Then get out of the situation with as little harm as possible.

If you are in a similar situation, take the confession at face value. Be glad you have the confession in hand. In fact, get the confession in writing, if possible. But then, keep looking, identify all of the areas the individual had access to and whether thefts could have occurred as a result. I'm willing to bet that you will find more losses than what was admitted to.

It is never my decision whether a client will prosecute or investigate further when confronted with this kind of information. Many choose to do nothing. Others choose to go forward with an insurance claim but never call the police. Others want the police involved at the outset. As we will explore in Chapter 13, there is no single right answer.

However, whether you're the owner or manager of a company, or the auditor or accountant advising a client, it is my experience that following through and investigating to the fullest possible extent gives my clients more peace of mind than those who choose not to look further. Many people have expressed regret for not following through and investigating the loss. Others have regretted not calling the police. It's often not enough for one's peace of mind to simply fire the fraudster and move on. The peace of mind does not come from an insurance claim and it does not come from calling the police. It seems that the peace of mind does come from knowing they looked into the issues and figured out "the number," whether or not they ever recoup those losses.

CHAPTER 10 NOTES

Certain displays of behavior are common before and after a fraud is discovered.

When faced with questions regarding anomalies, fraudsters will have plausible explanations, knowing that no documents will be reviewed.

Conversely, they may attempt to make the questioner feel bad for asking the questions in the first place.

Once caught, behaviors include denial, crying, acknowledgment of some level of wrongdoing, and negotiation for payback without calling the police.

PART IV

Prevention and

Recovery

Chapter 11

TONE AT THE TOP

A PRIVATE COMPANY CALLED US IN TO INVESTIGATE THE management in their US office before they went public in Japan. There were a few reports of expense reimbursements being incorrect, but it went unquestioned for a long time because the company was making good money. We combed through two years' worth of expense reimbursements for the top three people in the office—the CEO and the two vice-presidents. During those two years, these three executives stole $2.1 million.

It wasn't like they weren't paid well—the VPs earned upward of $400,000 per year and the CEO earned more than $500,000. Despite their great salaries, they charged a whole lot to the company: breakfast at McDonald's on their way to work, concerts, hotel suites, tennis lessons for the kids, holiday meals catered by the local country club, and vacations. The three of them took a trip together, and one expensed the tickets while the second expensed the hotel and the third expensed the meals. On that one weekend trip alone, they spent $28,000 at night clubs.

With our initial investigation completed, we were asked to take a look at the five people who were working under those three individuals. We sorted through the same two-year period of time and noticed that those five deputies had pretty clean records. The expenses for business trips, meals, and entertainment were totally reasonable and backed up by receipts and explanations of the expenses. Slowly, though, it seemed they started down that slippery slope. Personal items began to show up on expense reports—electronics, family meals, and personal vacations. It really wasn't surprising to see that the people who approved these expense reports were the CEO and the two VPs. It seemed that the unofficial office motto was, "Everybody's doing it, so I might as well do it, too."

One can find many definitions of "Tone at the Top." Typically, it is used to describe an organization's general ethical environment or management's leadership and commitment toward openness, honesty, and ethical behavior. According to the Association of Certified Fraud Examiners, there is a correlation between a company's Tone at the Top and its fraud risk.

If you walk into an office, you can feel the tone, or energy, of the organization. Are people working collaboratively, generally happy, and communicative? Conversely, are people stressed, are doors closed, and does there seem to be a general feeling that people are scared of management? Whether it's a healthy situation or whether it's uncomfortable and stressful, tone is something people can feel, and the tenor of the environment shows itself in the product of the work. The tone of a company is also critical to an organization's risk for fraud.

The trickle-down nature of the fraud we uncovered at the American subsidiary of a Japanese company is a glimpse into how the behaviors of management can adversely affect fraud risk.

Mark Whitacre, commonly referred to as "The Informant," was convicted of stealing five million dollars from his company, ADM Midland, while also acting as an informant for the FBI related to an international price fixing scheme. It was such an interesting story that it was adapted into a film. Mr. Whitacre, in an interview with the ACFE, states that the previous CFO stole eight million dollars, and when auditors caught him, he was simply asked to leave. The CFO kept his stock options, the company car, and his retirement benefits. Whitacre, with his knowledge of the price fixing scheme and the CFO's significant fraud, knew that corruption was widespread, and he knew that when the company found out he was acting as an FBI informant, he'd lose his job. Whitacre describes that he perpetrated the fraud to ensure that he'd have a "safety net" once he was eventually fired. He goes on to say that he figured there would be no negative consequences to stealing money from the company. After all, the worst that happened to the former CFO was a job loss, company car, stock, and a retirement package. There was little to no incentive not to steal.

On a smaller scale, a CPA friend of mine received a new client referral who wanted his tax returns done. The client was a business owner and angry that his former CPA hadn't caught the bookkeeper stealing from his company. When the bookkeeper was confronted, she looked at the owner and said, "You put your wife's department store expenses, her car, and the kids' tuition through the company books." Then she turned to the former CPA and said, "And you know it. You let him run all those personal expenses through the business, and he deducted it on his tax returns."

She pointed to the owner and said, "You're committing tax fraud," and turning to the CPA, she said, "And you're helping him do it."

The woman explained to them that she decided that if the owner and CPA were doing it, then why couldn't she?

The new CPA asked the owner if he wanted to get things back on track, and he said, "No, I'm still running that stuff through my business." Of course my CPA friend turned down the potential new client.

Whatever the tone is at the top of an organization, it trickles down to every employee, customer, and vendor. If the CEO or the owner of a company is misusing company funds, the payroll manager might decide she deserves a little extra padding on her next paycheck. If a company is cooking the books to make its quarterly goals and receive bonuses, then someone else might decide it's fair to skim a little cash off the incoming revenue. When the person at the top—the face or the role model of an organization—doesn't seem to have the health and well-being of the company in mind, it would be easy for others to take the hint and start looking out for themselves by whatever means necessary.

> *In fact, according to the ACFE's 2016 Report to the Nations on Occupational Fraud and Abuse,[viii] poor Tone at the Top was cited as one of the primary internal control weaknesses present when fraud was uncovered.*

Fortunately, the opposite is also true. When there is a really great, ethical tone at the helm of a company, that will also trickle down. This often takes the form of open-door management, where communication flows both ways and management wants to hear what's going on with the people who work for them. It's a more collaborative way of working, where there is more follow-through, better resolution, and more streamlined practices.

Tone at the Top is not a "one size fits all" definition for all organizations. Just as each organization is unique, so too are the strategies to implement a positive tone. Typically, a positive or healthy Tone at the Top includes the following:

---

viii   ACFE, *Report to the Nations on Occupational Fraud and Abuse*, p. 47.

- Open-door communication between management and lower level staff

- Management follows through on reports of conduct breaches

- Standard of ethical behavior is communicated, displayed by management, and expected of employees at all levels (i.e., ethics does not apply only to the lower level staff)

- Support programs for employees (e.g., mental health, substance abuse, financial counseling, etc.)

- Surprise audits

- Management oversight over processes and procedures

- Employees are expected to arrive to work on time, not to leave early, and to be productive during working hours

- Mechanisms for positive feedback are in place and used frequently

- Low turnover of management and staff

- Employees receive ongoing training and opportunities for advancement

- Hotline, or other mechanism to report anonymous tips, is in place and working

- Participation is required in the event of an internal or external audit or investigation

If everyone at a company is expected to follow the rules and it is made clear that fraud will be investigated and punished, an important first step has been established. If allegations of wrongdoing are reported, investigating those breaches of conduct is a way to encourage employees to say something when they see something. Even if no wrongdoing has occurred but staff knows that management has oversight over processes and procedures, such a tone can be a deterrent to fraud. And if fraud or other breaches of conduct are discovered, it is critical that appropriate sanctions be handed down.

Establishing an environment with that kind of follow-through has a better chance of reducing risk of employees committing thefts, as they may determine that the consequences of those sanctions outweigh the benefits of perpetrating a fraud. Refusing to investigate a fraud and giving the fraudster his or her retirement, stock options, and car leaves employees thinking, *If the guy who stole millions gets all those benefits, then what's the worst that can happen to me?* If a fraud is investigated and the fraudster goes to federal prison and is stripped of his retirement benefits, then naturally, people will think twice about the consequences of fraud.

When we finished investigating the extent of Linda's fraud, the owner, Bill, told us to sit tight while he called the police. Karen and I heard him on the phone saying, "No, no, don't send a plain clothes detective. Send me the biggest deputy you've got, and don't have him park back here in accounting. Have him park up front, and we'll meet him up there." He hung up the phone and guided us out of the office to the front of the building, to a large open room where approximately fifty people sat at separate cubicles. The cubicle walls around each desk were low so people could see one another, and us, as we walked up front.

The sheriff's office did not disappoint. They sent the biggest guy they had. When the officer arrived, he wore a radio on his shoulder, a belt with equipment, and a gun holstered to one side. He was a large presence, and when he moved, all of that gear shook and made noise. We stood with Bill beside the front desk as he introduced himself and us. Instead of walking down the side hallway to the accounting department, Bill escorted the deputy and Karen and me through the middle of the sea of cubicles. It was impossible not to look, and it was almost embarrassing to have everyone in the office staring at the mini-parade going by.

We were really confused as to what Bill was doing, and when we reached the hallway, Karen asked, "Bill, what was that all about?"

He said, "I want everybody to know that if they steal a single penny from me, that this guy is the one who is going to show up and arrest them."

The deputy took down our information, saying we needed to talk to a detective because that wasn't exactly his role. Bill asked, "Are you going to arrest her?"

"Based on what I'm seeing she will probably get arrested."

"Do you think you can go pick her up and have a handcuffing ceremony right here?" Bill asked.

Most people laugh when I tell that story. It's clear that Bill wanted to show everyone that he was adamant about following through on allegations of fraud. The remarkable thing about Bill's method was his ability to communicate to his staff without saying a word. The staff wasn't outwardly told why Linda was no longer at work, and I was never introduced to the staff as a fraud investigator. Clearly, the staff knew that something was amiss, with Linda being gone and an "auditor" asking questions and digging through documents. However, Bill wanted to make sure he had all the information and facts available to him before he made a statement or demonstrated the consequences of Linda's actions. Though the staff did not see the extent of the work we performed during our investigation or even know the total amount of funds she had taken, Bill seared the image of the deputy in their minds as what would happen if they attempted to steal from his company like Linda did. The level of follow-through in this case was really impressive and ended with Linda going to federal prison for four years.

There is no substitute for a positive ethical tone inside an organization. It is a key component in reducing fraud risk.

CHAPTER 11 NOTES

A healthy and positive tone at the top is directly correlated to an organization's risk of fraud.

Risk of fraud is low when a company's tone at the top is found to be positive.

A negative tone at the top can increase a company's risk of fraud.

Chapter 12

SEGREGATE DUTIES AND ESTABLISH INTERNAL CONTROLS

T HERE ARE TWO REASONS INTERNAL CONTROLS ARE PUT into place: to keep assets safe and to keep people safe in their jobs. We never want to see someone lose his or her job as a result of allegations that cannot be proven, and we never want to see someone seize an opportunity to commit fraud. Segregation of duties is one of the best practices for any company, and its importance comes close on the heels of setting the right tone at an organization. If a positive Tone at the Top is the overarching goal or strategy, segregation of duties is the more focused tactic.

When we ensure that one person doesn't have too much control over processes or procedures within a company, we significantly reduce the risk of fraud. Internal controls, specifically, segregation of duties, decrease the risk of somebody stealing money and increase the probability that fraud will be caught if it does occur. Separating duties ensures that more people are involved in the process and that there is appropriate oversight on the backend of each transaction.

I have worked with organizations both large and small and can typically find opportunities for improvement. Often, my clients will believe appropriate internal controls were in place, only to find they have eroded over time. I encourage you to assess the controls at your organization to determine whether appropriate segregation of duties, software controls, and processes and procedures are in place to reduce your risk of fraud.

This chapter is not meant to be a study on all of the controls that an organization can place over its employees in each department (that would be an entire book on its own!). Instead, it is meant to be a reminder of general concepts as they relate to the most common processes any organization sees on a daily basis. In the event that you need assistance determining whether your organization has appropriate controls, call your CPA or get a referral for a forensic accountant. It will be the best "insurance" you buy for your company.

Cash Receipts

Every business is different in how it brings in money. Businesses might bill clients at the end of the month, or process transactions through a cash register at the time of sale, or—in the case of a nonprofit or church—wait for donations. Regardless of where the money comes from, it is important to ensure that there are multiple people overseeing the entire process. We don't want a single person collecting the money, preparing the deposit, and taking the money to the bank. When an individual has that level of control over every step of the cash receipt process, then she has the opportunity to steal the funds, credit the customer account, or even act like the sale never happened.

If you have money coming into an organization—whether it's through a cash register, front desk, electronically, or through the mail, make sure that:

- Checks are endorsed immediately.

- There is a receipting mechanism, using pre-numbered receipts, for all sales or collection of funds.

- Person billing customers should not also collect funds and post payments.

- Person collecting money and posting to customer accounts should not also have the ability to place a credit or make a write-off to a customer's account.

  · This person should prepare a bank deposit slip and route a copy of it to the bank reconciler.

- Person who collects the money should be separate from the person who takes the funds to the bank.

  · Person who takes the funds to the bank should route the finalized bank deposit slip or receipt to the bank reconciler.

- Cash drawers should be segregated and accessible by only one employee per shift.

- Enforce cash shortage policies.

- Customer statements are not sent by individuals involved in handling incoming cash receipts.

- Bank reconciliation is not conducted by individuals involved in posting or taking cash to the bank.

  · Bank reconciler verifies the count sheet and the bank receipt match. Discrepancies should be investigated immediately.

NOTE TO SMALL BUSINESSES: I understand that you may not have the resources to employ several individuals in your accounting department. As such, this increases your need to find creative ways to segregate duties or ensure additional oversight on the back end of cash transactions.

Examples include,

- *Non-accounting employee takes the money to the bank.*

- *Print and review a detailed customer write-off or credit report each day (or week, or month) to ensure that no inappropriate credits were posted (run this report yourself, or have someone not involved in the posting of payments run this report).*

- *Ask your outside accountant to spot-check daily count sheets or pre-numbered receipts with bank deposits to ensure that all funds received were deposited to the bank.*

Nonprofits should consider that they are unique in that they typically do not generate sales or accounts receivables. Instead, they are often reliant on donations made, creating a situation where incoming funds are not expected or trackable. If you are involved with a church or nonprofit organization where you receive significant amounts of your revenue from donations, then at least two unrelated people should be charged with handling incoming cash or mail at all times. Otherwise, the person who receives the money might bank on the fact that no one else knows exactly how much money was received in the first place.

There's a small retail store in Seattle with only three registers to process approximately one thousand customers per day.

At the beginning of every shift, the drawer is counted by the cashier to ensure that it's at the correct amount for the day. At the end of each day, all of the drawers are counted by the closing manager to ensure that the cash balances match the registers' receipts. The owners personally count each cash deposit and bring it to the bank themselves.

Above each register is a small camera pointing down at the drawer. This way, if a register is short at the end of the night, or if a customer disputes the amount of change given, the security tapes may be reviewed to resolve the situation. Though the marketplace processes a fair amount of cash, there have been no known instances of cash skimming among cashiers, as they know they are being watched. Additionally, cashiers aren't able to void more than one item per transaction, and they are not able to process returns or refunds. A shift supervisor or manager has to scan a keycard in order to process refunds.

There are at least three people running checks and balances at this small marketplace to ensure that the amount taken in matches the deposits. The cashiers count their drawers, the closing manager compares the transactions and final balances, and the owner counts the deposit and brings it to the bank. In this way, fraud is significantly deterred.

 Understanding and verifying your cash receipt process is important, too. Sometimes, organizations believe an appropriate process is in place, only to find that a fraud still occurs despite their best efforts. A non-profit client of mine found a loophole in their cash receipt system the hard way. They had pre-numbered sequenced receipts. Each day, the office manager would count the receipts and the cash received the night before. Only trouble was, she "needed" some of that money and would help herself to the cash, taking out the corresponding receipts as well. They thought they had a good system of checks and balances because the office manager would route the receipts and the funds to the front desk clerk who would recount the money and the receipts and prepare the funds for deposit. Unfortunately for my client, no one thought to train the front desk clerk to ensure that all of the receipts were in sequence and that none were missing. Had this simple step been included in her daily process, the office manager's fraud would have been discovered on the first day, instead of many years and tens of thousands of dollars later.

In short, someone should always double-count the money to verify that it matches sales reports or cash registers, and someone else should be taking that to the bank. Finally, someone else should be reconciling these reports to the bank deposits at the end of each month. Knowing who is responsible for what helps to ensure that there's no one area ignored or a loophole found where someone could easily take the money without detection.

Check Disbursements
Most businesses, large and small, pay their bills through the check disbursement process. And whether you issue a handful

of checks per month or thousands, appropriate segregation of duties and internal controls is the same.

- New vendors should be approved by management and entered into the accounting system by someone other than the accounts payable clerk.

- New vendors should be researched via an onsite visit or via your state's business registry office to ensure the vendor is not owned by an employee of the paying company.

- Invoices from vendors should be approved by the appropriate level of management prior to entry into the accounting system.

- The person signing checks should not be the person who can approve the invoices and/or enter the invoices into the accounting system.

- Checks should only be signed if they are supported by an approved invoice.

- Checks should be mailed by someone other than the accounts payable clerk.

- Bank reconciliations should be performed by someone other than the accounts payable clerk.

- Consider using your bank's positive pay system to ensure that only checks to approved payees clear your account.

- If wire transfers are used to pay bills, ensure that there are dual controls in place whereby one employee sets up the wire transfer and a separate employee, using separate and distinct log-in credentials, approves and sends the wire.

- Ensure that all canceled check images are returned with your monthly bank statement and are reviewed consistently each month.

NOTE TO SMALL BUSINESS: *The single most important line of defense you have is the review of your bank statement and canceled check images each month. Make sure your bank statement is routed to someone other than the person preparing and processing your checks (you, your spouse, your outside accountant, a non-accounting employee, etc.). Train that person to review the front of the statement for any unauthorized electronic withdrawals and to review the canceled check images for inappropriate payees and amounts.*

In addition, consider the following:

- *Ensure that all checks are signed by you or an authorized designee and are supported with vendor invoices.*

- *Ask your outside accountant to perform the monthly bank reconciliations.*

- *When reviewing the bank statements and canceled checks, ask your bookkeeper/accountant to pull documents for specific transactions. Even if you know the answer, the perception that you are conducting a thorough review is critical to reducing your fraud risk.*

- *Never sign blank checks.*

Oftentimes, small companies will allow bookkeepers to have check-signing authority because the owner is so busy. Many people think this is more efficient, but for the sake of efficiency we hand people the keys to the kingdom and give them the opportunity to steal. Some clients say, "There's not enough money here to steal." Sadly, many a client has suffered losses under that incorrect assumption. If there is even five dollars in the bank, there's money to steal.

Debit or Credit Card Disbursements

If debit or credit cards are distributed to employees, make sure that you have appropriate policies that incorporate rules around spending, ATM withdrawals, etc. Some banks offer companies the ability to ban purchases from certain establishments (e.g., liquor stores, bars or clubs, online retailers, etc.).

In the event that employees carry debit or credit cards, ensure that:

- Daily and monthly spending limits are in place and monitored.

- All receipts must be retained by the employee and remitted before the end of each month.

- All charges are summarized on an expense form, with the date, amount, vendor, and purpose of the charge.

- All charges must be reviewed and approved by an appropriate-level supervisor.

- Reconcile employee receipts and expense forms to monthly debit or credit card statements.

  - Reconciliation must include verification that vendors paid matches information provided by the employee.

- Employees are aware of oversight over the debit and credit card charges in that questions are asked and/ or additional information is obtained.

Payroll

If you have a business, you likely have employees. And whether you process your payroll in-house or with an outside company, you have risk associated with this function. Best practices related to payroll include:

- Segregating the hiring and human resources function from the payroll function.

- Payroll hours are approved by appropriate level of management before hours are entered into the payroll system.

- Paid time-off hours are related to a set benefit for all employees and usage is approved by management before being entered into the payroll system.

- Use a direct deposit system to pay employees (instead of paper checks).

- Ensure that all tax and retirement withholdings are remitted to appropriate regulatory agencies at the same time payroll is processed.

- If using paper checks, rotate who distributes paper checks on pay day.

- Review payroll reports each pay period, once payroll is processed.

NOTE TO SMALL BUSINESS: One of the most common ways I see small businesses being victimized is the failure of their bookkeepers to pay payroll taxes. The non-payment of the payroll taxes effectively gives the fraudsters "more money" to steal. And given that the IRS and state agencies will send paper notices in the mail, the non-payment of the taxes can go on for years before it is uncovered. When it comes to payroll, consider the following:

- *Use your CPA firm or an outside agency to process your payroll, payroll taxes, and payroll tax form filing.*

- *Review payroll reports once payroll has been processed by in-house employees or your payroll services.*

- *Verify that employees are not taking more paid time off than allowed per company policy.*

- *Verify that employees are not being paid overtime or additional hours that were not earned.*

Expense Reimbursements

In the event that employees are allowed to use their own credit cards to incur business-related debt, ensure that you have appropriate polices in place that describe allowable expenditures and requirements for receipts. Similar to debit and credit card charges, internal controls should include:

- All receipts must be retained by the employee and remitted before the end of each month.

- All charges are summarized on an expense form, with the date, amount, vendor, and purpose of the charge.

- All charges must be reviewed and approved by an appropriate-level supervisor.

- No reimbursements will be made without an original receipt (i.e., credit card statements cannot be presented as proof of a charge).

- Employees are aware of oversight over the debit and credit card charges in that questions are asked and/ or additional information is obtained (e.g., compare their calendars with their travel-related charges).

Segregation of duties and internal controls work best when employees understand the importance of their roles; when they understand that implementation of these strategies are not due to their untrustworthiness, but rather because we want to keep them safe in their jobs; and when management has a system for continuous monitoring or oversight.

While a positive Tone at the Top reduces fraud risk overall, appropriate segregation of duties and functioning internal controls is one of the most effective strategies in detecting and deterring fraud.

CHAPTER 12 NOTES

The implementation of internal controls, specifically the segregation of duties, is the best way an organization can deter fraud.

Consider some of the ideas in chapter 12 to verify whether there are opportunities to improve internal controls at your organization.

In the event that you need more assistance, your local CPA or forensic accountant would be happy to assist you in conducting a more formal assessment.

It is the best "insurance" your company can buy!

Chapter 13

To Prosecute or Not

THE DECISION TO PROSECUTE IS ONE OF THE FIRST QUES-
tions my clients ask me. It is also the decision that they
struggle with the most. Usually, the discovery of the fraud has
just happened, the extent of it is unknown, and people are
distraught, emotional, and often disbelieving. When you've
never expected that fraud could occur at your company, it's
hard to fathom next steps. Thankfully, the decision to prosecute does not need to be made immediately. Most states
have a statute of limitations, and it's important to know the
statute in your state. In Washington, for instance, it's three
years from the discovery of the crime; so, a client typically
has plenty of time to make this difficult decision.

There are a few reasons why clients don't want to prosecute,
the first being that they feel it's embarrassing as a business
owner to be the victim of fraud. They often turn it on themselves, asking, "What's wrong with me that I trusted this
person?" Prosecuting can mean that the ordeal becomes
public knowledge, and my clients fear the public humiliation.

The second reason is the reputation of the business. Will business be negatively impacted if this story is on the front page of the local newspaper? What will clients and customers think? Will it influence sales? This is a real concern for a non-profit organization that relies on donations to fuel its operations. It is not uncommon for donations to diminish when it is perceived the organization cannot handle or manage donated funds. On the other hand, I have never had a business client call and say their business did poorly because the story was on the front page of the newspaper. Many stories won't be printed at all. Of the handful that make the paper, those clients have called and told me that people reached out to them to say, "I'm so sorry this happened to you." Often others will admit to my clients that it happened to them years ago, too. Many clients find that instead of losing business or being shamed by the community, they receive genuine and empathetic responses.

Finally, most people wouldn't dream of making another person's life terrible. Fraudsters are often the most trusted and well-loved employees, so it can be hard to accept that they've committed fraud and even harder to prosecute someone you know and trusted. Owners and managers know that the fraudster is a wonderful spouse or parent, that he or she has a family, and a reputation to uphold. Many don't want to be seen as the person who ruins a family or a reputation.

According to the ACFE's *2016 Report to the Nations on Occupational Fraud and Abuse*, approximately 40 percent of known fraud cases were not referred to law enforcement.[ix] The primary reason was the fear of bad publicity.

REASONS CASE NOT REFERRED TO LAW ENFORCEMENT

Source: ACFE 2016 *Report to the Nations on Occupational Fraud and Abuse*, Figure 102, Page 76.

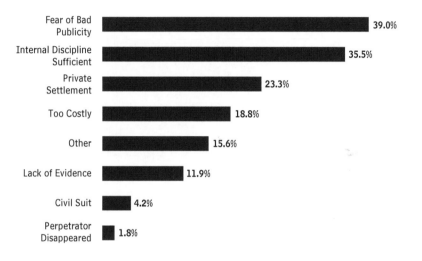

My own kids were very young when I worked on Linda's case, and the morning after she was arrested, I remember thinking that she woke up in jail that day. I looked at my kids and husband and thought, *I can't imagine any amount of money being worth waking up in jail,* and expressed that thought to my husband. When my six-year-old heard that, he said, "Mommy, you sent somebody to jail?" I'll never forget how he looked at me, confused and upset. I explained that it wasn't my fault that this person went to jail, but that her decision to

---

ix   Ibid., pp. 75 and 76.

steal led to her arrest. It was simply my job to tell the police and judge what happened.

No one wants to be the person who feels she has ruined someone else's life. One of the hardest things to remember in the middle of it all is that these are not usually isolated incidents. It's not uncommon to hear that people who are let go for theft go on to steal from their next employer. Many of my clients have been victims of serial fraudsters—some of whom had not been prosecuted or the prosecution fell through. As an example, when Karen and I had our first meeting with the sheriff's detective, he slid a picture of Linda across the table to us. I had never seen her before and asked whether this was her DMV photo. He laughed. He told me it was her booking photo from when she had been charged with stealing from her previous employer in an adjacent county.

Reporting someone may diminish his or her chances of getting a job, but it will also diminish the chances of him or her committing fraud at another company—plus, lower the risk of fraud at your own organization after she has left.

Knowing that every situation is different and every organization has various needs, I never discourage or encourage my clients from prosecuting. People often think it's my job to report the crime, but it isn't. A fraud investigator's job is to determine exactly what happened and inform clients of the particulars so that they can make an informed business decision. Ultimately, the client has to decide what's best for the organization. I tell my clients the facts and what my experience has been with other clients, both those who decided to prosecute and those who decided not to. Instead of advocating for a certain course of action, I express that I am sorry for what they are going through, and a decision does not have to be made right away. It's best to figure out exactly what happened first, quantify the losses, and determine the length of time the scheme has occurred. Those facts help people make sound decisions. I also encourage my clients to look at their bylaws and other governing documents for the organization. For instance, when I work with nonprofits, they often have very specific rules, which may include a requirement to call the police if they find fraud. This takes the emotional decision out of the hands of the board of directors and puts it into the governing documents.

Aside from understanding the size and scope of the situation and knowing relevant bylaws, it's really important to know what the process of prosecution actually looks like. That way, people can decide whether or not it's the route they need to take.

If you call the police, usually a detective will come and speak with you. Based on the merits of what you tell him or her, the detective will likely call dispatch to receive a case number for a potential theft. Things could stop there. Once you have called and received a case number, you've often met the minimal requirements of an insurance policy.

If you decide you want to prosecute the case, regardless of where you are in the United States, you cannot always rely on local law enforcement to have the resources to investigate the full extent of the case. This is critical to understand. Most law enforcement agencies are constrained by budget resources and caseloads. What's more, fraud cases are document intensive. It takes a lot of time to compile a financial crimes case. Most local law enforcement jurisdictions don't have the resources to devote their time to doing this. Likewise, many law enforcement officers have not been trained in the nuances of accounting or financial crimes. I've worked with a wide range of law enforcement departments over the years, and many of them say that they'd rather work on property crime, domestic violence, or homicide crimes than a financial crime. These types of cases take a lot of time, energy, and comprehension of numbers.

As such, it has been my experience that when a client puts together a case for law enforcement, it is more likely to get prosecuted. In my experience, whether the fraud you are dealing with will be prosecuted at the local or federal level, there are key factors that will lead to the success of the prosecution.

Make the Case

When clients pay to have a forensic accountant put a case together, they exponentially increase the chance that the local police or sheriff will investigate the crime. However, putting the case together is more than just making a report or giving law enforcement a pile of documents.

In order to make your case, you first must have the sufficient relevant evidence to prove the loss occurred. Do you have canceled check images that prove your employee wrote checks to himself? Do you have copies of receipts that prove funds came in and never made it to the bank? Does your accounting system show that manipulations occurred, specifically at the hands of the suspect?

Based on the sufficient, relevant evidence, you must minimally pull together a set of schedules that quantify the loss. It is my recommendation that you present your case to law enforcement with a narrative report that can "stand alone" without your or your forensic accountant's presence. Remember, this report will be seen by detectives, prosecuting attorneys, defense attorneys, a judge, and potentially a jury—and you will not always be there to explain it. The report should include the quantification of the loss, the source documents you relied on to prove the loss, background related to the case in terms of how the fraud was uncovered, and the reasons why you believe no other individual benefited from the lost funds.

Ideally, you will present your report, supporting schedules, and the corresponding evidence in an organized and well-marked fashion. This reduces the amount of work necessary for law enforcement and the prosecutor who will be assigned to your case.

In the event my clients have limited resources and cannot afford for us to put the case together for them, I will typically advise them to use a combination of our resources and their own to put the case together. Their staff's time can be used to perform the time-intensive (and often costly) tasks that involve identifying and copying bank statements and other documents and creating simple schedules of loss amounts. We have used this "resource combination" successfully many times. With Linda's case, my client hired a temporary employee and he was tasked with reviewing all of the bank statements and canceled checks and verifying which check images were missing. From that list, we ordered the check images from the bank, and nearly all of them turned out to be for the benefit of Linda. The temporary employee then listed the date, check number, payee, and amount of each of the returned checks and made copies of them for me. I was able to rely on his work and focus my efforts on other investigative tasks, including interviews, report write-up, and working with my clients to unravel the impacts of the fraud on their accounting records.

It is important to note that a single report, whether written by you or your forensic accountant, can serve multiple purposes. It can be used for insurance claim purposes, civil proceedings, or a criminal prosecution. In other words, you don't need three different reports for three different purposes—one should suffice.

Don't Include the Kitchen Sink

Every fraud case will include nuances; there will be losses that are easy to identify as attributable to the suspect, while others will be "questionable." It is imperative that your case includes only those losses that you can prove. Many clients will want to put all loss figures in as if they are related to the fraud, when in reality they may not be. The most common issue I find is when we have debit or credit card charges to big-box stores like Costco, Target, or Walmart without any corresponding receipts. If we know that the organization buys office supplies at these stores, then we can't automatically assume all of the charges to these stores are fraud-related losses, in the absence of receipts.

In my experience, my clients often have very specific loss figures attributable to the suspect. Whether those losses are payroll related, thefts of cash receipts that can only be explained as benefiting the suspect, or checks written to or for the benefit of the suspect, it is my experience that these direct losses are the only kinds of losses necessary for the report.

The "kitchen sink" types of losses, the ones that cannot be definitively proven or refuted as fraud related, should remain out of your case. They can be mentioned in your report. They can even be quantified. But it is not my recommendation that they be included as the amounts attributable to the fraud-related loss.

As someone who also works on behalf of defendants and who has had her fraud reports scrutinized by many a defense attorney, it is always best to include only what you can prove. You do not want your case to be perceived as inaccurate, vindictive, or embellished. Typically, the "kitchen sink," or questionable loss figures, will not mean the difference between whether or not your case is prosecuted, or whether or not the suspect will face restitution or jail time.

Notify and Involve Law Enforcement Early

Once you decide that prosecution is the way you want to go, make the call to your local law enforcement (or FBI) office and ask to make an appointment with a detective. Be prepared for your meeting by having some pertinent information ready, including:

- The name of the suspect

- The suspect's date of birth and/or Social Security number

- A brief background of how you discovered the fraud (dates, people involved in the discovery, etc.)

- Your findings to date

- Examples of evidence you have (e.g., canceled checks)

- Your proposed deliverable (i.e., report, schedules, and marked evidence binder)

The detective will provide you with valuable direction for your case. He may ask questions you had not thought about and need to get the answers to. He may be able to take some of your findings to date and start his own investigation by talking to those involved or issuing search warrants on the fraudster's bank accounts. Once you have your case put together and delivered it to the detective, he will be in a much more knowledgeable position to perform his own investigation and recommend it for charging and prosecution.

Be a Pest

Even under the best of circumstances, law enforcement officers may take time to investigate your case. Locally, I have had many white-collar cases be set aside when a homicide or other major crime occurs because the detectives are pulled into major crime cases. In other circumstances, I know that local law enforcement's caseloads are burdensome and hard to manage.

Whatever the difficulties facing law enforcement, I encourage my clients to give the detectives several weeks to get started on the case. They will know when the investigation gets started, calls will be made, interview appointments will be set up, and eventually, my clients will be informed that an arrest or charging document is imminent.

In other circumstances, the case just gets buried. I have found that clients who call every week or two to inquire about their case often have results or information more quickly than those who do not. In other words, the squeaky wheel gets the grease!

Sometimes, inquiries have revealed that the detective buried the case because he or she could not make heads or tails of what the client originally produced. Similar to the case involving Jerri, we have been hired to put the case together and resubmit to law enforcement because my clients were unaware of the time and resource constraints of their local law enforcement officials, and initial submissions were not sufficient for a crime to be charged or prosecuted.

Once the case is charged out, a similar pattern will often repeat itself at the prosecuting attorney's office. And my clients once again need to make regular phone calls to inquire about the status of their case.

It is important to note that "being a pest" does not equate to yelling or demeaning. It is simply a recommendation to communicate to local law enforcement officials that your case is important to you, has had a significant financial and emotional burden on you, and that you wish for it to be properly investigated and prosecuted.

In fact, the more collaboratively you can work with law enforcement and prosecuting attorneys, the more successful the outcome of your case will be.

My clients have various reasons why they choose to call the police and why they choose not to. Some of the common reasons they do call the police involve their belief in the criminal justice system and "doing the right thing."

Others want to set a specific tone at their organization, like Bill. After all, classic criminology theory teaches that swift, public punishment will deter the person from doing it again and deter others in the organization from repeating someone's actions.

In addition to setting the tone, deciding to prosecute means that you can potentially establish a criminal record for the perpetrator. In some instances, law enforcement will report that the fraudster already has a history of fraud (an indication your company could step up background checks). The person may or may not go to jail if you prosecute, but there will be a greater chance that the crime perpetrated against you will be on his criminal background history. If he goes on to apply for another job and the organization runs an appropriate background check, his known history makes it less likely he will be able to commit fraud again. A company may choose not to hire him or it might hire him but ensure his access to assets is restricted.

You should note that once you hand your case over to law enforcement, it is out of your hands and you will have very little to zero control over the outcome.

My clients are often appalled that the person is charged with fewer counts of theft and/or losses less than those proven in their report. The way that a defendant is charged and the amount of loss he or she is charged with is subject to a number of factors and is different in each jurisdiction.

Charges do not always equate to handcuffs. In some instances, the fraudster will be arrested and may even have to spend a night or weekend in jail before being arraigned. In other instances, he is given a court date and must simply appear in court on his own volition.

The suspect will retain a defense attorney or be assigned a court-appointed one. From there, the defendant will most likely plead not guilty during an arraignment proceeding. Typically, these individuals are set a bail amount, and they often walk free from the courthouse that day. Also during the arraignment, an initial trial date may be set. The "not guilty" plea provides the defendant and his attorney time to thoroughly review the charges and any discovery in the case (i.e., your report and schedules, the supporting documentation, and the detective's interview memos).

It is typical for my clients to ready themselves for the first trial date, fretting over whether they will be called as witnesses, how they will feel seeing the person again, and whether or not the trial will be covered in the newspaper. What they don't realize is that the likelihood the case will go to trial on that date is small. Typically, the initial trial date will be "set over" and will not take place.

It is during this time that the clients may become aware that the prosecuting attorney's office is discussing the case with the defendant's attorney and offering a plea deal. Plea deals can include negotiations on the number or type of crimes charged, the recommended restitution, and the recommended jail time. Plea deals are normal and customary during this process. Many of my clients are assigned a victim's advocate and are consulted during the whole process. They don't necessarily get to make the ultimate decision but are consulted regarding the plea deal negotiations.

To date, I have testified in only a single criminal trial. Many white-collar criminal cases are settled during the plea deal process and are never decided by a jury.

Typically, the culmination of a criminal proceeding, whether adjudicated through a plea negotiation or via a jury decision, is the sentencing hearing. This is the time and place for the judge to impose sanctions in the form of jail time and restitution on the defendant. It is also the time and place for my clients to tell the judge the impact of the person's actions—emotionally and financially.

In some cases, the defendant will be handcuffed and placed in custody that day. In other cases, the defendant will report for jail time at a date determined by the judge.

On average, once a client has reported a crime to law enforcement, it takes at least one year for the entire process described above to take place. In one instance, the process took less than six months from the report to the FBI to the defendant's sentencing. In another instance, the process took five years. The caseload of law enforcement and the prosecuting attorneys' offices, the requests for additional time by the defense attorneys, the complexity of the case, and the overfull dockets of the court system can all factor into the speed with which a case will be prosecuted.

Last, do not expect that a prosecution experience will equate to restitution being paid to you. It is only in rare cases that defendants have the cash or other assets to repay my clients for losses suffered. Usually, the cash is gone, and there are no assets for the government to seize. While restitution is often ordered, my clients are typically disappointed that the amounts do not come close to recouping losses. I will never forget when Bev and Christine called me after receiving Lynn's first restitution check from the Washington State Women's Penitentiary. They wanted to take me out to "celebrate."

"Awesome! Where are we going?" I asked cheerfully. They told me they received a check for $17, so we'd have to find a place with "really cheap margaritas on a happy hour menu." Given the fact that their company lost in excess of $450,000, a payment plan of $17 per month would not pay off the debt in my clients' or Lynn's lifetime.

CHAPTER 13 NOTES

The choice to prosecute is often a deeply personal one for victims. Unless they are bound by governing documents, a host of financial and emotional considerations are part of the ultimate decision.

If the choice to prosecute is made, it is more likely that a case will be investigated if it is put together by the victim or the victim's forensic accountant.

Expect that once the prosecution process commences it will take at least one year to see it to the end and sometimes much longer.

While defendants are often required to pay restitution, clients often find that installment payments will never come close to being sufficient for losses sustained.

Chapter 14

I Found Fraud! Now What? Ten Steps

"Take a deep breath." It may sound a bit more touchy-feely than the advice you might get from your typical accountant. But it's the first piece of advice I give all potential clients who call me after they've discovered a fraud. It's the first thing people need to do when they discover fraud is occurring at their company. When fraud happens, it's totally overwhelming, as if you have tangled Christmas lights you can't unravel. One can feel completely helpless in the face of it—as if this company you thought you had control over is sliding out of control. I see my job as giving power back to the people who have been victims of fraud. I help them untangle the situation so they can feel in control and able to move forward again. The reason I ask people to stop and take a deep breath is because they need to be as clear-headed as possible so they can navigate what's coming. There are a lot of decisions on the horizon.

The first of the ten steps to dealing with fraud is to understand that it's not going to be figured out or resolved overnight but that it will eventually be figured out over time. Emotions will run high, and a calming breath will help you prevail.

Second, grab a legal pad and write down key events and communications. When we're stressed or emotional, we forget the sequence of events or the details. Writing everything down can help you remember and keep track of when things were uncovered and how. Otherwise, it's easy to forget who was called or who said what to whom. All you need is a simple legal pad or notebook. Write down who told you what, how you uncovered the fraud, who you called, when you had conversations with the suspect, and what those conversations entailed. Also, document any conversations with key witnesses, your attorney, or insurance agent. Write down the dates of conversations, and keep adding to the log of events as you remember information. It doesn't have to be neat—there is a multi-faceted reason for this exercise. It will help you clear your mind and get it out of your head and onto the page. That documentation can also be handed to a forensic accountant for critical information on case background. Or it can be referred to when speaking with the police. Law enforcement and accountants will ask for this critical background information to understand what happened, why, and when.

The third step is to secure the computer and facility access of the suspect in question. Many people work remotely or use mobile devices like cell phones and tablets. All phones, computers, tablets, and electronic devices need to be collected. If the suspect has remote access, e-mail addresses, or log-ins that she can reach from another computer, then disable her ability to access those. If she has physical access to the building, either through keys or a card system, then have her return the keys, change the locks, and/or disable her card access.

The fourth step is to secure computers or electronic devices in a safe. Do not turn on the computer. Definitely do not repurpose a computer for a new employee. Just take all of those items, store them in a safe, and ensure that no one has access to them. Steps three and four are important because we don't want the suspect or anyone else destroying evidence—deleting files, changing information, or shredding documents. There could be critical evidence on the electronic devices that have been confiscated, and giving the computer to another employee to repurpose it could inadvertently destroy evidence. I've worked on cases where the person who has been fired or laid off will ask her coworkers to go into her desk or computer to destroy or remove evidence from the premises. Treat this time frame as a triage emergency mode, and don't trust anyone just yet.

When the devices are securely stored, back up the company's computer system. Many systems run a backup every night, but you'll need to segregate the backup for that night in particular and store a copy in the safe.

The fifth step is to secure key documents: bank statements, canceled checks, financial statements, vendor invoices, deposit slips, receipts, payroll reports, and other intellectual property. Whatever seems pertinent to a case based on the current evidence needs to be collected and secured because you'll need those documents to build and prove a case.

The sixth step is to contact key individuals. If you're a manager, then you may want to contact the owner or CEO of the business. Depending on the organization, this might be something you do after step two, once you've written down everything you can remember about the situation. The owner or CEO can serve as an ally and help you secure computer and facility access and key documentation.

The seventh step is to contact legal counsel and the insurance company. If clients do not already have legal counsel, I send them the names of three local employment law attorneys, so they are able to make a choice about who can best represent them. Employment law issues are critical in fraud cases, from whether to put a person on administrative leave to whether to terminate employment, to whether to confront her with the situation or just let her go. If the accused is a union employee, additional legal considerations must be addressed. In addition, having legal counsel can also protect some of the work product of your forensic accountant as the case is being investigated. Legal counsel is a critical resource to have and to be able to confer with in all steps of the process. Their advice will not cost as much money as you may think, and their wise and level-headed counsel will often serve in providing peace of mind.

Once you've established legal counsel, call your insurance agent or company and ask whether you have employment dishonesty insurance or a fidelity bond. If so, ask what the policy limits are. Does your policy cover professional fees for forensic accountants or your legal counsel? There are a lot of insurance companies that will cover some or all of the fees, and it's important to understand your policy limits and coverages before you move forward with the investigation.

The eighth step is to begin to think about the end game. This does not mean you have to make a decision about whether or not to prosecute, but this is the point of the process where I ask my clients a few questions. Will termination of an employee or multiple employees occur? Is prosecution a possibility? Is an insurance claim going to be filed? Understanding or envisioning the end game or intended outcome is imperative to properly scope and navigate the investigation and to ensure that appropriate counsel and experts are contacted and consulted. Though nothing needs to be set in stone, these questions need to be considered.

The ninth step is to consult a forensic accountant—not your regular accountant. Forensic accountants have the specific knowledge to properly conduct an investigation. They know the proper procedures, how to collect evidence, how to write reports, and how to provide expert witness testimony.

The tenth and final step is to mitigate the risk moving forward. Educate your staff to understand the risk of fraud and how to recognize and report key indicators and suspicious behavior. Ensure you have appropriate internal controls and proper segregation of duties.

The goal of these ten steps is to give you peace of mind and provide a framework in which to work. When fraud is discovered, the impact to an organization and its employees is far-reaching, and it's hard to know exactly what to do. Things can feel out of control. These simple steps will help you move forward, regain control, and take clear action toward finding out what happened and why. Once these ten steps have been taken, the investigation can begin in earnest. It's a lot easier to begin an investigation once a client feels more in control and ready to confront the situation.

When I worked from home, I sometimes ended the workday a few hours early to spend time with my family. Once, on a Friday at three o'clock, I was leaving my home office when the phone rang. Trying to be better about balancing work and home life, I decided to let it go to voice mail. When I reached the kitchen, my cell phone rang with a call from the same number. Again, I let it go to voice mail, but as soon as my husband and I started chatting about our weekend plans, the home phone rang. When he answered, the voice on the other end of the line sounded troubled.

My husband said, "I understand. I'm so sorry. Hold on. I'll

see if she's available." Everyone on my staff and in my family knows to apologize to a client if they call for me and are distressed about potential fraud losses. When he turned to me, he said it was the same woman who called the office and my cell—that she had found my name in the white pages and in desperation called our home phone. She caught her bookkeeper stealing from her earlier in the day and was clearly distraught.

"Where's your office?" I asked. "Can I come there?"

She calmed down on the phone, but by the time I arrived at her office, she was all worked up again. She was joined by her mother, who had once owned the business, and her accountant. The desk was piled high with documents. The owner cried, saying she had trusted and loved this woman but just found out that she was coming to work drunk and stealing money.

Finally, I said, "I totally understand what's going on, but we are not going to fix this today." She stared at me, and I continued. "Don't get me wrong, we will fix this. We will figure out what happened here, but that's not going to happen today. It's 4:15 on a Friday. We do not have time to unravel this right now. I'm taking the weekend off, and you're taking the weekend off, too."

"I can't take the weekend off," she said. "My business is in shambles."

"What do you like to do on the weekends?"

Confused, she answered, "Ride horses."

"Do you drink wine?"

"Heck, yeah, I drink wine."

"Here's what you're going to do. You're going to go home. You're going to ride your horse. Then you're going to drink a glass of wine. You're going to take the whole weekend off, and do whatever it is you like to do on weekends. On Monday morning, I will meet you back here at nine o'clock. We will sit down and figure this out then."

"But I need something to do this weekend," she said.

"Take out a yellow pad of paper and write down the sequence of events. I want to know what happened, when you hired her, how you found out about what happened, and what documents you think we're going to need to figure this out."

She nodded.

"Does this woman have keys to the building?" I asked. "Can she access e-mail over the weekend or any of the computers from home?"

"No," the owner said.

"Great. Then the only thing you're going to do is write down the sequence of events. Otherwise, ride your horses and drink your wine."

"Can I go to church?" she asked.

"Church is probably a great place to go."

"I'm not sure I'm ready to forgive her," she said.

We all had a good laugh, and she seemed a little calmer, so I added, "We are not going to fix this over the weekend. When we meet again on Monday, you're going to be in a much better frame of mind. We are going to be able to deal with the rest of this."

When she didn't respond, I asked, "Are any of these documents going anywhere?"

She shook her head.

"Is this woman going to go anywhere?"

"I guess she could."

"Yes, she could, but we can find her, wherever she is in the world. That's not going to change what happened."

"Okay," she said. She suddenly looked serene. "It's 4:30. We're going to close the office, and I'm going to go home and ride my horses."

The owner took two days off, rode horses, drank a bit of wine, went to church, and told me on Monday that she felt so much better. She was ready to confront the situation. We determined that the bookkeeper stole $10,000, which was a significant sum for the business but not significant enough to cause permanent damage. It was the emotional aspect of realizing that a trusted and loved employee had betrayed her that had her feeling so distraught. Once she had taken the weekend to process it, she was ready to face the facts, which weren't that bad, all things considered.

To me, this was a routine case, but to her, my simple suggestions made their own impact. I once heard her tell a group of professionals at a cocktail party, "I was totally over the edge, didn't know which end was up, didn't have any control over my thoughts, and didn't know what to do next." That weekend, she said, "I would get upset and cry about what this woman had done to me, but then I remembered what Tiffany told me to do. So I went for long rides on my horse, I ended the day with a bubble bath and some wine, and then I would go back to the yellow pad of paper and write down the sequence of events. By the time I got to work on Monday, I was able to be clear and deal with it. I handed the details over to Tiffany and went back to running my business. Before that weekend, I was so upset, I couldn't even run my business."

Fraud has a way of turning our worlds upside down and suddenly throws into question everything we've been doing. Dealing with the emotional aspect of these crimes first is the only way out of the morass you will find yourself in. From there, following small but simple steps will help you to regain control. Only then, with clarity and peace of mind, can you move forward with confidence.

CHAPTER 14 NOTES

1. Take a deep breath.

2. Log all communications and events.

3. Eliminate computer and facility access.

4. Secure a server backup and all electronic devices in a safe. Do not reuse or repurpose devices.

5. Secure key documents.

6. Contact owners and management.

7. Contact legal counsel and insurance agent.

8. Think about the end game.

9. Consult with a forensic accountant.

10. Mitigate risk going forward.

The Thief in Your Company

IF YOU FIND YOURSELF IN A SITUATION WHERE YOU BELIEVE you are or may be the victim of fraud, I am truly very sorry. Please understand that this is not your fault. Somebody used his or her ability to be liked and trusted to perpetrate a crime against you, and no one deserves that. It is likely that the Thief in Your Company was literally just that, not only an employee but also someone you kept close to you, was perhaps even a member of your inner circle. Whatever you are going through—whether it's anger, embarrassment, confusion, helplessness, guilt, or sadness—is normal, and you are not alone in feeling this way. Though it may feel like it, you are also not alone in this situation. There is help available.

Unfortunately, fraud happens. It happens on a daily basis. Every day, nice people just like you realize they are victims of fraud and run through the gamut of emotions you are currently facing. You are not alone in how you feel. It is possible to figure out what happened and move forward. Whether or not you decide to prosecute, figuring out what happened will give you peace of mind and clarity, which you can carry forward in perpetuity.

If fraud has occurred at your workplace, it doesn't have to happen again. As you understand who commits these crimes and the situations that lend themselves to an increased risk of fraud in your organization, you will seek out those situations and mitigate risks by ensuring you have appropriate internal controls, segregation of duties, and oversight.

Similarly, if you have not been a victim of fraud and want to avoid it happening in your organization, there are ways to help ensure that it doesn't happen to you. There are resources in this book to assist companies in setting up proper systems to mitigate fraud, and your local CPA or forensic accountant can help you with a plan tailored for your business.

Finally, understand that while trust is a foundation in most human relationships, it cannot be the foundation upon which you implement controls around your employees. As we have gleaned from the unfortunate situations my clients found themselves in, it is often implicit trust that is the breeding ground for fraud to occur. It is the very people my clients liked and trusted the most who perpetrated the frauds against them. We need to build a foundation of trust between employers and employees, but it can only be built when employers commit to proper oversight and controls, and when employees feel protected and secure in their jobs.

Even with all of that, an employment-based relationship must always come with a safety net called verification.

If you're an auditor, manager, or business owner, it's really important to understand the human elements of financial crimes. Fraudsters look like us and act like us. They become indispensable and much-loved employees who are members of the inner circle. When fraud is uncovered, we must first deal with the emotional impacts. The loss calculations should be secondary.

We must also remember that the fraudster's esteemed status and reputation will deter whistleblowers who perceive themselves as "less than." As auditors, managers, and owners, we need to leave space for whistleblowers to approach us. Listen, be open, and follow through on what whistleblowers have to say.

It's important to understand the nuances of who is perpetuating these crimes, and how they get around it—not just on a technical plane but in the way their interpersonal relationships allow them to continue.

It is my hope that this book and my clients' stories will give you the courage to take the necessary precautions to keep your organization's employees and assets safe, or to look into that situation that has been bothering you for a long time. I promise you, taking these steps will ultimately allow you to focus on what you do best: running your business.

About the Author

TIFFANY COUCH, CPA/CFF, CFE, IS PRINCIPAL AT ACUITY Forensics, a Pacific Northwest forensic accounting firm with a national presence. She has more than 19 years of experience in the field of accounting, with the last 12 years focused completely on forensic accounting–related engagements. Ms. Couch holds a bachelor of science degree in accounting, *cum laude*, from Central Washington University, as well as the professional designations of Certified Public Accountant (CPA), Certified in Financial Forensics (CFF), and Certified Fraud Examiner (CFE).

Her professional background and experience include audit, tax, and business consulting services for government entities and privately held business entities in a range of industries, including aerospace, agriculture, automotive, banking, biotechnology, broadcasting, computer technology, construction, health care, insurance, manufacturing, newspaper, professional service providers, retail, timber, and transportation.

Ms. Couch is the winner of the 2014 James R. Baker Speaker of the Year, presented by the Association of Certified Fraud Examiners (ACFE) to honor an individual who has demonstrated the true spirit of leadership in communication, presentation, and quality instruction.

Ms. Couch was elected by the general membership of the ACFE to serve on the Board of Regents for the two-year term of 2015 and 2016, serving as chairwoman of the board in 2016.

She has provided expertise as a source to the *New York Times, The Wall Street Journal, National Public Radio,* and *First Business News.* She is also a regular contributor to *Fraud Magazine* and the *Vancouver Business Journal.*

Ms. Couch is an honoree of the 2007 Accomplished & Under 40. Community businesses and agencies recognize their rising stars in this event, which is hosted by the *Vancouver Business Journal.* Acuity is a three-time winner of the *Vancouver Business Journal's* annual Business Growth Awards:

the 2007 Start-Up Business of the Year and the 2008 and 2009 Fastest Growing Business in the 1–5-year category. This event recognizes fiscal year growth of southwest Washington's top companies.

Ms. Couch resides in the southwest Washington area with her husband and two sons.

For more information about Ms. Couch, please visit *www.tiffanycouch.com.*

For more information about Acuity Forensics, please visit *www.acuityforensics.com.*

Glossary

ACCOUNTS RECEIVABLE – Money owed to a business from its customers or clients as a result of the delivery of products or services. [5]

ACCOUNTS RECEIVABLE AGING – A periodic report that categorizes a company's accounts receivable according to the length of time an invoice has been outstanding (i.e., unpaid). [5]

ASSET MISAPPROPRIATION SCHEME – A scheme in which an employee steals or misuses the employing organization's resources (e.g., theft of company cash, fraudulent disbursement schemes, or theft of physical assets).[3]

ASSOCIATION OF CERTIFIED FRAUD EXAMINERS (ACFE) – The world's largest anti-fraud organization and premier provider of anti-fraud training and education.[3]

AUDIT TRAIL REPORT – Paper or electronic trail that gives a step-by-step documented history of a transaction.[4] In many accounting systems, the audit trail report will provide the reader with information that includes the date and time a transaction was entered, changed, or deleted; the user name of the individual who entered, changed, or deleted the transaction; as well as the dollar amount and accounts affected by the transaction and/or its changes.[6]

BALANCE SHEET – The balance sheet is a report that summarizes all of an entity's assets, liabilities, and equity as of a given point in time. It is typically used by lenders, investors, and creditors to estimate the liquidity of a business.[2]

BANK RECONCILIATION – A bank reconciliation is the process of matching the balances in an entity's accounting records for a cash account to the corresponding information on a bank statement.[2]

BILLING SCHEME – A fraudulent disbursement scheme in which a person causes his or her employer to issue a payment by submitting invoices for fictitious goods or services, inflated invoices, or invoices for personal purchases.[3]

BUDGET – An estimation of the revenue and expenses over a specified future period of time.[5]

CASH LARCENY SCHEME – A scheme in which an incoming payment is stolen from an organization after it has been recorded on the organization's books and records (e.g., employee steals cash and checks from daily receipts before they can be deposited in the bank).[3]

CASH RECEIPT – The collection of money (currency, coins, checks). Not to be confused with revenues.[1] A cash receipt can also be described as a printed statement of the amount of cash (i.e., currency, coins, checks, credit card payments) received in a cash sale transaction. A copy of this receipt is given to the customer, while another copy is retained for accounting purposes.[2]

CASH SKIMMING SCHEME – A scheme in which an incoming payment is stolen from an organization before it is recorded on the organization's books and records (e.g., employee accepts payment from a customer but does not record the sale and instead pockets the money).[3]

CHANGE ORDERS – Unilateral written order by a project owner directing the contractor to change contract amount, requirements, or time. Such changes must be within the scope of the contract and in accordance with the contract's changes clause to be legally implemented without the consent of the contractor.[4]

CHECK TAMPERING SCHEME – A fraudulent disbursement scheme in which a person steals his or her employer's funds by intercepting, forging, or altering a check or electronic payment drawn on one of the organization's bank accounts.[3]

COST OF GOODS SOLD – The accumulated total of all costs used to create a product or service that has been sold.[2]

DEPOSITION – Recorded out-of-court testimony of a witness, or before a magistrate or judge, to obtain discovery of facts or for use in a trial. [4]

EXPENSE REIMBURSEMENT SCHEME – A fraudulent disbursement scheme in which an employee makes a claim for reimbursement of fictitious or inflated business expenses (e.g., employee files fraudulent expense report claiming personal travel or non-existent meals). [3]

FINANCIAL STATEMENT FRAUD – A scheme in which an employee intentionally causes a misstatement or omission of material information in the organization's financial reports (e.g., recording fictitious revenues, understating reported expenses, or artificially inflating reported assets). [3]

FRAUD – In the broadest sense, fraud can encompass any crime for gain that uses deception as its principal modus operandi. More specifically, fraud is defined by *Black's Law Dictionary* as "A knowing misrepresentation of the truth or concealment of a material fact to induce another to act to his or her detriment." Consequently, fraud includes any intentional or deliberate act to deprive another of property or money by guile, deception, or other unfair means. [3]

FRAUD RISK – An organization's vulnerabilities to internal and external fraud. [3]

FRAUD TRIANGLE – Donald Cressey's model for explaining the factors that cause someone to commit occupational fraud. It consists of three components which, together, lead to fraudulent behavior. One leg of the triangle represents a perceived non-shareable financial need. The second leg is perceived opportunity, and the third is rationalization.[3]

FRAUDULENT DISBURSEMENT SCHEME – Making a distribution of company funds for a dishonest purpose. Examples of fraudulent disbursements include forging company checks, the submission of false invoices, doctoring time cards, and so forth.[3]

GHOST EMPLOYEE SCHEME – A perpetrator might use a fictitious employee placed on the payroll to generate fraudulent paychecks. The ghost employee might be an ex-employee kept on the payroll after termination, a newly hired employee on the payroll before employment begins, or a completely fictitious person.[3]

INCOME STATEMENT – An income statement is a financial statement that reports a company's financial performance over a specific accounting period. Financial performance is assessed by giving a summary of how the business incurs its revenues and expenses through both operation and non-operating activities. It also shows the net profit or loss incurred over a specific accounting period.[5]

INTERNAL CONTROLS – An internal control is a process, effected by an entity's board of directors, management, and other personnel, designed to provide reasonable assurance regarding the achievement of objectives relating to operations, reporting, and compliance. [3]

JOURNAL ENTRY – A journal entry is a formal accounting entry used to identify a business transaction. The entry itemizes accounts that are debited and credited and should include some description of the reason for the entry, as well as the date. [2]

LAPPING SCHEME – Lapping occurs when an employee steals cash by diverting a payment from one customer, and then hides the theft by diverting cash from another customer to offset the receivable from the first customer. This type of fraud can be conducted in perpetuity because newer payments are continually being used to pay for older debts, so that no receivable involved in the fraud ever appears to be that old. [2]

LEDGER – A book or database in which double-entry accounting transactions are stored and summarized. The ledger is the central repository of information needed to construct the financial statements of an organization. [2]

MATERIALITY – Usually refers to statements that are sufficiently important or relevant to a reasonable person in acting or making a decision. [3]

MATERIALLY MISSTATED – The accidental or intentional untrue financial statement information that influences a company's value or price of stock.[7]

OCCUPATIONAL FRAUD – The use of one's occupation for personal enrichment through the deliberate misuse or misapplication of the employing organization's resources or assets.[3]

PAYROLL SCHEME – A fraudulent disbursement scheme in which an employee causes his or her employer to issue a payment by making false claims for compensation (e.g., employee claims overtime for hours not worked; employee adds ghost employees to the payroll).[3]

SHELL COMPANY – Refers to a company that has no physical presence and generates little or no independent economic value.[3]

SOURCE DOCUMENTS – Source documents are the physical basis upon which business transactions are recorded. Source documents are typically retained for use as evidence when auditors later review a company's financial statements and need to verify that transactions have, in fact, occurred.[2]

TONE AT THE TOP – Tone at the Top refers to the ethical atmosphere that is created in the workplace by the organization's leadership. Whatever tone management sets will have a trickle-down effect on employees of the company.[3]

Glossary Sources

1   ACCOUNTING COACH

2   ACCOUNTINGTOOLS.COM

3   ASSOCIATION OF CERTIFIED FRAUD EXAMINERS

4   BUSINESSDICTIONARY.COM

5   INVESTOPEDIA

6   TIFFANY COUCH/ACUITY

7   VENTURELINE.COM

30781102R00140

Made in the USA
San Bernardino, CA
29 March 2019